First World War
and Army of Occupation
War Diary
France, Belgium and Germany

5 DIVISION
15 Infantry Brigade
Bedfordshire Regiment
1st Battalion
1 April 1918 - 20 April 1919

WO95/1570/3

The Naval & Military Press Ltd
www.nmarchive.com
Published in association with The National Archives

Published by

The Naval & Military Press Ltd

Unit 10 Ridgewood Industrial Park,

Uckfield, East Sussex,

TN22 5QE England

Tel: +44 (0) 1825 749494

www.naval-military-press.com

www.nmarchive.com

This diary has been reprinted in facsimile from the original. Any imperfections are inevitably reproduced and the quality may fall short of modern type and cartographic standards.

© **Crown Copyright**
Images reproduced by permission of The National Archives, London, England, 2015.

Contents

Document type	Place/Title	Date From	Date To
Heading	WO95/1570/2		
Heading	15th Brigade 5th Division 1st Battalion Bedfordshire Regiment April 1918		
Heading	War Diary of 1st Bedfordshire Regt For The Month Of April 1918		
War Diary		01/04/1918	30/04/1918
Operation(al) Order(s)	Operation Order No.132 1st Battalion Bedfordshire Regiment	01/04/1918	01/04/1918
Miscellaneous	April 1918		
Operation(al) Order(s)	Operation Order No.133 1st Battalion The Bedfordshire Regiment	01/04/1918	01/04/1918
Miscellaneous	April 1918 App I		
Operation(al) Order(s)	Operation Order No.134 1st Bn Bedfordshire Regiment	03/04/1918	03/04/1918
Operation(al) Order(s)	Operation Order No.135 1st Bn Bedfordshire Regiment	09/04/1918	09/04/1918
Operation(al) Order(s)	Operation Order No.137 1st Battalion The Bedfordshire Regiment.	16/04/1918	16/04/1918
Operation(al) Order(s)	Operation Order No.138 1st Battalion The Bedfordshire Regiment.	20/04/1918	20/04/1918
Miscellaneous	Headquarters 15th Infantry Brigade Reference Proposed Minor Operation	23/04/1918	23/04/1918
Operation(al) Order(s)	Operation Order No.139 1st Battalion The Bedfordshire Regiment.	25/04/1918	25/04/1918
Miscellaneous	Report On Attack And Taking Of Enclosure At K.21.a Reference Attached Sketch Map	26/04/1918	26/04/1918
Operation(al) Order(s)	Operation Order No.140 1st Battalion The Bedfordshire Regiment.	26/04/1918	26/04/1918
Miscellaneous	Headquarters 15th Infantry Brigade	27/04/1918	27/04/1918
Miscellaneous	Appendix 9	28/04/1918	28/04/1918
Heading	1st Bedfordshire Regt May 1918		
Miscellaneous	British Salonika Force War Diary		
Heading	War Diary of 1st Bedfordshire Regt For The Month Of May 1918		
War Diary		01/05/1918	31/05/1918
Miscellaneous	Warning Order	02/05/1918	02/05/1918
Operation(al) Order(s)	Operation Order No.141 1st Battalion The Bedfordshire Regiment.	08/05/1918	08/05/1918
Miscellaneous	May 1917		
Operation(al) Order(s)	Operation Order No.142 1st Battalion The Bedfordshire Regiment.	15/05/1918	15/05/1918
Operation(al) Order(s)	Operation Order No.143 1st Battalion The Bedfordshire Regiment.	28/05/1918	28/05/1918
Heading	1st Bedfordshire Regt June 1918		
Miscellaneous	British Salonika Force War Diary		
Heading	War Diary of 1st Bedfordshire Regt For The Month Of June 1918		
War Diary		01/06/1918	30/06/1918
Operation(al) Order(s)	Operation Order No.145 1st Battalion The Bedfordshire Regiment.	12/06/1918	12/06/1918
Operation(al) Order(s)	Operation Order No.146 1st Battalion The Bedfordshire Regiment.	18/06/1918	18/06/1918

Operation(al) Order(s)	Operation Order No.147 1st Battalion The Bedfordshire Regiment.	21/06/1918	21/06/1918
Operation(al) Order(s)	Operation Order No.148 1st Battalion The Bedfordshire Regiment.	23/06/1918	23/06/1918
Operation(al) Order(s)	Operation Order No.149 1st Battalion The Bedfordshire Regiment.	30/06/1918	30/06/1918
Heading	1st Bedfordshire Regt July 1918		
Miscellaneous	British Salonika Force War Diary		
Heading	War Diary of 1st Bedfordshire Regt For The Month Of July 1918 Vol 45		
War Diary		01/07/1918	31/07/1918
Operation(al) Order(s)	Operation Order No.151 1st Battalion The Bedfordshire Regiment.	04/07/1918	04/07/1918
Operation(al) Order(s)	Operation Order No.152 1st Battalion The Bedfordshire Regiment.	11/07/1918	11/07/1918
Operation(al) Order(s)	Operation Order No.153 1st Battalion The Bedfordshire Regiment.	16/07/1918	16/07/1918
Operation(al) Order(s)	Operation Order No.154 1st Battalion The Bedfordshire Regiment.	19/07/1918	19/07/1918
Operation(al) Order(s)	Operation Order No.156 1st Battalion The Bedfordshire Regiment.	23/07/1918	23/07/1918
Operation(al) Order(s)	Operation Order No.157 1st Battalion The Bedfordshire Regiment.	29/07/1918	29/07/1918
Heading	1st Bedfordshire Regt August 1918		
Miscellaneous	British Salonika Force War Diary		
Heading	War Diary of 1st Bn Bedfordshire Regt For The Month Of August 1918		
War Diary		01/08/1918	31/08/1918
Operation(al) Order(s)	Operation Order No.158 1st Battalion The Bedfordshire Regiment.	05/08/1918	05/08/1918
Miscellaneous	Aug 1918		
Operation(al) Order(s)	Operation Order No.159 1st Battalion The Bedfordshire Regiment.	07/08/1918	07/08/1918
Operation(al) Order(s)	Operation Order No.160 1st Battalion The Bedfordshire Regiment.	13/08/1918	13/08/1918
Operation(al) Order(s)	Operation Order No.161 1st Battalion The Bedfordshire Regiment.	16/08/1918	16/08/1918
Operation(al) Order(s)	Operation Order No.162 1st Battalion The Bedfordshire Regiment.	20/08/1918	20/08/1918
Heading	1st Bedfordshire Regt September 1918		
Miscellaneous	British Salonika Force War Diary		
Miscellaneous	Headquarters 15th Infantry Brigade.		
Heading	War Diary of 1st Bedfordshire Regt For The Month Of September 1918 Vol 47		
War Diary		01/09/1918	30/09/1918
Operation(al) Order(s)	Operation Order No.163 1st Battalion The Bedfordshire Regiment.	01/09/1918	01/09/1918
Operation(al) Order(s)	Operation Order No.164 1st Battalion The Bedfordshire Regiment.	04/09/1918	04/09/1918
Operation(al) Order(s)	Operation Order No.165 1st Battalion The Bedfordshire Regiment.	14/09/1918	14/09/1918
Operation(al) Order(s)	Operation Order No.166 1st Battalion The Bedfordshire Regiment.	20/09/1918	20/09/1918
Miscellaneous	Notes on Enemy Trenches And Territory Opposite IV Corps Front	23/09/1918	23/09/1918
Miscellaneous	Standing Administrative Instructions for Battle	23/09/1918	23/09/1918

Type	Description	From	To
Miscellaneous	Information From Aeroplane Photographs	24/09/1918	24/09/1918
Operation(al) Order(s)	15th Infantry Brigade Operation Order No.220	24/09/1918	24/09/1918
Miscellaneous	Addendum To 15th Infantry Brigade O.O No.221	25/09/1918	25/09/1918
Miscellaneous	In Connection With The Forthcoming Attack The Major General Wishes To Impress The Following Points on All Commanders	25/09/1918	25/09/1918
Operation(al) Order(s)	15th Infantry Brigade Operation Order No.221	25/09/1918	25/09/1918
Operation(al) Order(s)	Operation Order No.147 1st Battalion The Bedfordshire Regiment.	25/09/1918	25/09/1918
Operation(al) Order(s)	Operation Order No.148 Battalion The Cheshire Regiment.	26/09/1918	26/09/1918
Miscellaneous	15 Infy Bde No. G.A.I	26/09/1918	26/09/1918
Miscellaneous	Operation Orders		
Miscellaneous	15th Infantry Bde	26/09/1918	26/09/1918
Operation(al) Order(s)	15th Infy Bde O.O No.223	29/09/1918	29/09/1918
Heading	1st Bedfordshire Regt October 1918		
Heading	War Diary of 1st Bedfordshire Regt For The Month Of October 1918		
War Diary		01/10/1918	31/10/1918
Operation(al) Order(s)	Operation Order No.168 1st Battalion The Bedfordshire Regiment.	09/10/1918	09/10/1918
Miscellaneous	Oct 1918		
Operation(al) Order(s)	Operation Order No.169 1st Battalion The Bedfordshire Regiment.	10/10/1918	10/10/1918
Operation(al) Order(s)	Operation Order No.170 1st Battalion The Bedfordshire Regiment.	11/10/1918	11/10/1918
Operation(al) Order(s)	Operation Order No.171 1st Battalion The Bedfordshire Regiment.	12/10/1918	12/10/1918
Operation(al) Order(s)	Operation Order No.172 1st Battalion The Bedfordshire Regiment.	19/10/1918	19/10/1918
Miscellaneous	Oct 1918		
Operation(al) Order(s)	Operation Order No.173 1st Battalion The Bedfordshire Regiment.	22/10/1918	22/10/1918
Miscellaneous	1st Battalion The Bedfordshire Regiment Addendum to Operation Order No.173 dated 22/10/18	22/10/1918	22/10/1918
Miscellaneous	Oct 1918		
Miscellaneous	5th Division Summary of Information	25/10/1918	25/10/1918
Miscellaneous	Report On Prisoners Captured During Recent Operations	25/10/1918	25/10/1918
Miscellaneous	British Salonika Force War Diary Anti-Aircraft Sections		
Heading	1st Bedfordshire Regt November 1918		
Heading	War Diary of 1st Bedfordshire Regt For The Month Of November 1918		
War Diary		01/11/1918	30/11/1918
Operation(al) Order(s)	Operation Order No.174 1st Battalion The Bedfordshire Regiment.	03/11/1918	03/11/1918
Operation(al) Order(s)	Operation Order No.176 1st Battalion The Bedfordshire Regiment.	03/11/1918	03/11/1918
Operation(al) Order(s)	Operation Order No.175 1st Battalion The Bedfordshire Regiment.	10/11/1918	10/11/1918
Miscellaneous	British Salonika Force War Diary Anti-Aircraft Sections		
Heading	1st Bedfordshire Regt December 1918		
Miscellaneous	British Salonika Force War Diary		
Heading	War Diary of 1st Bedfordshire Regt For The Month Of December 1918		
War Diary		01/12/1918	31/12/1918

Operation(al) Order(s)	Operation Order 177 1st Battalion The Bedfordshire Regiment.	12/12/1918	12/12/1918
Miscellaneous	Dec 1918		
Heading	War Diary of 1st Bedfordshire Regt For The Month Of January 1918 Vol 51		
War Diary	Gembloux	01/01/1919	31/01/1919
Heading	War Diary of 1st Bedfordshire Regt For The Month Of February 1919		
War Diary	Gambloux	01/02/1919	07/04/1919
War Diary	Gilly	08/04/1919	17/04/1919
War Diary	Antwerp	18/04/1919	20/04/1919
Operation(al) Order(s)	Operation Orders No.179 1st Battalion The Bedfordshire Regiment.	16/04/1919	16/04/1919
Operation(al) Order(s)	Operation Orders No.178 1st Battalion The Bedfordshire Regiment.	06/04/1919	06/04/1919
Heading	15 Infantry Brigade 1 Battalion Bedfordshire Regiment 1914 Aug To 1919 Apr		

WD 95/15/70/2

15th Brigade.

5th Division.

---o------------

1st BATTALION

BEDFORDSHIRE REGIMENT

APRIL 1918.

From ITALY

CONFIDENTIAL.

Register.........
Part No........
Volume No......

WAR OF DIARY

1st Bedfordshire Regt.

for the month of

April

---------1918.

K.Williams
CAPTAIN,
STAFF CAPTAIN,
15TH INFANTRY BRIGADE.
for R.C.
Commanding

Army Form C. 2118.

WAR DIARY
or
INTELLIGENCE SUMMARY
(Erase heading not required.)

Instructions regarding War Diaries and Intelligence Summaries are contained in F. S. Regs., Part II. and the Staff Manual respectively. Title Pages will be prepared in manuscript.

Place	Date	Hour	Summary of Events and Information	Remarks and references to Appendices
April	1st/4/18		Battalion billeted at CREOLA. Training carried on. Lt. Col. E.J. a. S. Hope D.S.O. returned from 75th Inf.y Bde. + resumed command of Batt. O.O. 133.	App. I
	2nd	—	Battalion marched to LONGARÉ and billeted.	
	3.	—	As above. Batt. preparing for entraining for France.	
	4.	—	B^n marched to TAVERNELLE. 1st Train consisting of "A" "C" Coys and ½ Transport, left at 10.10 p.m. Personnel of 2nd train bivouaced for night. O.O. 132.	App. II
	5.		Second train left TAVERNELLE at 6.15 a.m. In trains en route for France.	
	6.		Route: MODANE, MÉONE, FONTAINEBLEAU, DOULONS. FRÉVENT.	
	7.		Both trains arrived at FRÉVENT, + detrained. Each train marched independently to NEUVELLETTE + billeted.	
	8.		As above.	
	9.		Marched to SOMBRIN, + billeted. O.O. 135. Batt^n in readiness to move off at ½ hours notice	
	10		Marched to SAULTY + entrained. Detrained at AYRE + marched to LAMBRES. Batt^n billetted with an outpost line around N part of village.	App. III

Army Form C. 2118.

WAR DIARY
or
INTELLIGENCE SUMMARY
(Erase heading not required.)

Instructions regarding War Diaries and Intelligence Summaries are contained in F. S. Regs., Part II. and the Staff Manual respectively. Title Pages will be prepared in manuscript.

Place	Date	Hour	Summary of Events and Information	Remarks and references to Appendices
April	12.		Battn. less Lewis Gun & bombers personnel, moved up to CROIX MARIAS. Brigade being Brigade in Support, to 40th Division. Battn. Bivouaced - carried out a day defensive position.	
	13.		Battn. Commenced digging Support Line (Divisional line) Damaged Personnel moved to TANNAY.	
	14.		B". Relieved the R.W.Rents in Divisional line. Work on line carried on every & improving trenches R. S. Casualties - 1 man killed, 5 wounded	
	15.		As above - Artillery fairly quiet. Casualties 1 killed 4 wounded.	
	16.		15th Infy Bde relieved 95th Bde in left sub. sector of Div. Front. Battn. Moved 12th Gloucesters in Support. O.O. 137. Lt. Col E.J. de S Thorpe D.S.O. to command 152 + Mr Bell as temp. Brigadier Maj M.M Halford. M.C. Gloster Regt. assumed command of Battn. As above. Casualties 1 killed 2 wounded	App 111
	17.		" " " 4 "	
	18.		" " " 1 "	
	19.		" " " 2 "	
	20.		Draft of 31 O.Rs to rein. Work done, wire in support. All Coys. built trenches RS. for protection in the wood. At night 2 Coys. moved into Brigade reserve line. Clouded upon - 2 Coys dug slits	

2449 Wt W14957/M90 750,000 1/16 J.B.C. & A. Forms/C.2118/12.

WAR DIARY or INTELLIGENCE SUMMARY

Army Form C. 2118.

Place	Date	Hour	Summary of Events and Information	Remarks and references to Appendices
April	20.		Assembly trenches.. E of wood.. to accommodate whole of 1st R.R. in case of alarm.. or gas.	
	21st		Battn. relieved 1st NORFOLK REGT in night Sub Sector - of 1st Bde Sect: OO/38. Several Casualties were caused later by Own Artillery firing Short. Casualties: 1 O.R. Killed & 4 O.R. wounded.	App V.
	22nd		Heavy Gas Shelling during night 21/22 - Enemy Fired T.M.s on front line. Casualties 2 O.R. Killed - 6 wounded.	
	23.		As above - large party of Enemy in front of Centre Coy. dispersed by L.G. & rifle fire & Arty Blue barrage - Active Patrolling Carried On - Lieut/2 on line returning on whole front. 2/Lt Johnson (6. Y.R.) D/Lt Hutchinson wounded.	App 6.
	24.		Rt. Coy (A. Coy) Preparing for Minor Operation (See App 6.) Officers Patrol Reconnoitred Ground for Minor Operation - Casualties - 3 O.Rs wounded.	
	25		A. Coy Supported by two Platoons of 'B' Coy. took all objectives as detailed in O.O.139. Zero hour 3.0 p.m. - All objectives reported taken by 10.35 p.m. - See App. 8. Capt G. F. Hague wounded - 1 O.R Killed Do O.R. attack wounded.	App 7. App 2.

WAR DIARY
or
INTELLIGENCE SUMMARY

Army Form C. 2118.

Place	Date	Hour	Summary of Events and Information	Remarks and references to Appendices
	25	midnight	Lt. A.H.O. Pickwell & E.J.Y. Miller, D.L.I., F.L. Ray joined Battalion.	
	26		Situation Quiet - 3 O.R.: wounded.	
	27		Enemy attacked right Coy at about 11-30 a.m. - Capt. R.M. White - wounded. 2/Lt. A.B. Peel killed. M.O.R. killed. 11 wounded. Battn. was relieved by 3 Coys. of K.O.S.B. & 1 Coy. of D.C.L.I. & withdrew to Camp in Wood - O.O. 140. -	Off. 9. Off. 10
	28		As above.	
	29		As above. O.O. supplied working party of 400 men to work on Divisional line, wiring & improving trenches.	
	30			

M. White
Commanding 1st Bn. Bedfordshire Regiment

App II

Operation Order No. 132.
1st Battalion Bedfordshire Regiment.
April 1st 1918.

1. Battalion will entrain at TAVERNELLE Station
Date. April 4th 1918. — Time — 10.11. p.m.

2. TRAINS. — Bn. will entrain in 2 trains: Each train will consist of:—
    1. First or Second Class Coach
    2. Third Class Coaches
   22. Covered Trucks.
   13. Flats
    2. Brake Vans. —

Bn will be distributed as under.
Train 1.   H.Q.   Serial No 534.
H.Q. Lt. Col. E.I. de S. Thorpe D.S.O. — A/Adjt., Transport Officer.
Quartermaster — Lt. T.P. Kingdom — Cpl. Law. —
H.Q Servants & Mess Staff — Cpl. Belben & 3. Pioneers. —
DRUMS. —
A & C. Coys complete :— 1. M.O. Orderly, 2 Orderly Room.
Half Transport. — 2. L.G. Limbers
                  { 1/2. Limber. S.A.A.
                  { 1/2   "   Bombs.
                  { 1/2   "   Tools.
                  { 1/2   "   Signalling

1. Water Cart, 1 Cooker, 1 Cooks waggon, 1 Baggage
1. Supply waggon — Mess Cart 4 Pack Animals.
Chargers of Officers, travelling on train. —

Train "B" – O.C. Train – Major C.H.W. Halford. M.C.
Medical Officer a/Major R.C. Mc M. Betty. R.C. Stanton
R.C.M. S. Transport Sgt. + 1. M.O. Orderly. –
Remainder of Transport – Maltese Cart, 3 Pack Animals. –
B & D. Coys Complete. L/Cpl Dudley + 3 Pioneers.
1. Barber. 1. Cutler.
N.B. All Headquarters Employ not Enumerated above
will travel with their Coys.
Q.M. Employ will travel with Transport.

3. Entraining Officer Capt. C.A. Warner M.C. 15th T.M.B.
   Detraining Officer. Capt. F.C. Pearman. M.C. D.W.R.

4. Entraining. – All animals & vehicles will arrive at the
   Entraining Station 3 hours before train is timed to
   start. Personnel will arrive 1 hour before.

5. Loading Parties. A party of 2 Officers & 100. O.R. from
   1st Norfolk Regt. will be detailed for loading at VICENZA.

6. Equipment & Rations. Each man will entrain carrying full
   equipment. 120 Rounds S.A.A. rations for day of Entrainment,
   Iron rations, full water bottle, steel helmet, box respirator
   & 2 Blankets. –
   All clipped animals will be rugged, other animals will
   have 1 rug each, carried on transport.

7. Forage. Forage for day of Entrainment will be carried
   in the horse trucks. Men in charge of horses will travel
   in the horse trucks. Supply wagons will be loaded full.

8. Animals. Animals will be entrained unharnessed. Harness
   will be loaded under its vehicle. Canvas buckets will be
   carried in each horse truck. Cinders or Gravel will be
   strewn on floors of horse trucks. –

Breast Ropes must be provided for all horses. No cats will be fed, for the 1st 12 hours after Entrainment.
Ventilation of Trucks is important, & should be regulated as to wether train is in motion or halted. The door on the side of running way, is to be kept closed.
Tins for carrying water up to 24 galls. per truck will be supplied at Entraining Station. Horses will be entrained by their own drivers.

9. <u>Rations</u>. 8 days rations, in addition to those mentioned in paras 6.&7. will be carried in bulk, for all men & animals on each train. A covered truck will be set aside for issue of rations En-route. Forage & non-perishable Supplies can be loaded under vehicles.
If possible bread will be issued en-route at "St Germain au Mont d'or". Forage for day of Entrainment will be carried in horse trucks. E.F.C. will arrange for a Canteen lorry to be at each Entraining Station.

10. <u>Discipline</u>. The strictest discipline will be maintained throughout the journey. The senior Combatant Officer will Command each train, & he will appoint Orderly Officers, who will take tours of duty & will also detail a guard at each end of the train of 1 N.C.O. & 3 men. The duties of Orderly Officers & guards are:—
(a) To see that no one leaves the train when it halts unless authorised to do so, at a recognised halting place by the O.C.
(b) To ensure that no men ride on the steps, or tops of carriages, or climb along the train from truck to truck. There is very little clearance between the trucks & Tunnel,

c. To guard all stores on train throughout.
d. To watch both sides of train when halting.
e. Each O.C. Train will obtain from the Entraining Officer before starting a copy of G.H.Q instructions for O.C trains. These instructions are secret & should be destroyed before detraining.

Cooking & fires of any description are forbidden in any horse trucks.

At halts the following signals by bugle will be given.
For everyone to leave the train – Regimental Call. & G.
Warning that train will move in about 5 minutes – Regimental Call. & "Fall In".
Warning that train will move immediatly – Regimental Call & Advance.

(11) Entraining States. – The O.C of Each train will send on in advance an Entraining State in duplicate. This state will shew strength of Officers, O.Rs, horses by types, vehicles by types, the number of days rations entrained. These states will be handed over to Entraining Officer. A Certificate will be added to the effect that the unit is complete with equipment & rations.

12. <u>Gas Drill</u>. During the journey, bose respirators will be worn for at least 1 hour daily. – by all ranks.

13. **Billeting**. A billeting party consisting of Capt. F. Hague & C.S.M. Hals will proceed by 1st train of Brigade Group S. They will take bicycles & report to Entraining Officer at VICENZA at 6 a.m. 16th inst.

Capt Hague will be responsible for billeting the Battⁿ in France. They will travel on No. 6 train from VICENZA reporting to Lt. Col. Deakin.

14. **Surplus Kit**. All surplus kit will be conveyed in 2nd train. It will be kept separate & orders will be issued at detraining Station, as to wether it is to be dumped there, or wether there will be transport available to take it to billeting area. —

S. H. Draper.
Lt & Adjt
1st Bⁿ Bedfordshire Regt.

April 1918

Operation Order No 133
1st Battalion The Bedfordshire Regt

April 1st 1918

1. On the 2nd inst. the Battalion will march to BANGANE. Battalion starting point - Church at CAESAR.
Order of March:
H.Q. to pass starting point at 10 A.M.
"B" Coy. -- -- -- 10.2 A.M.
"A" Coy. -- -- -- 10.4 A.M.
"D" Coy. -- -- -- 10.6 A.M.
"C" Coy -- -- -- 10.8 A.M.
Transport -- -- -- 10.10 A.M.

Drums will march with "D" Coy.

2. BLANKETS - Blankets will be rolled in bundles of 10. "A" & "B" Coys. & H.Q. will take Blankets to Q.M's Stores by 7 A.M. "C" & "D" Coys will have blankets ready for collection by 7 A.M. Officers' kits, Mess kits, & books kits will be ready for collection at 8 A.M.

3. PROTECTION AGAINST HOSTILE AIRCRAFT
As on march from BADOERE. "A" & "B" Coys. will find reserve L.G.s # 1 & 2 to accompany them to report to T.O. by 9 A.M.

4. MARCH DISCIPLINE - Dress, intervals etc. as on previous march.

S. H. Hooper-Lieut & Adjt
1st Bn Bedfordshire Regt

Copies to
1 C.O.
2 13th Infy Bde
3 A Coy.
4 B Coy.
5 C Coy.
6 D Coy.
7 T.O.
8 Q.M.
9 M.O.
10 Lt. & Mo M Betty
11 " J.P. Kingdon
12 File
13 G.S. War Diary
16 R.S.M.

April 1918

App I

Operation Orders No 134 / 13

1st Bedfordshire Regiment.
3rd April 1918

(1) On the 4th inst. Battalion will march to TAVERNELLE Station to entrain. — Battalion Starting point - ROAD JUNCTION 500 yards N. of B in LONGORE

Order of March: A Coy will pass Starting point 2 p.m.
                 C ,,   ,,   ,,   ,,   2.2 p.m.
                 B ,,   ,,   ,,   ,,   2.4 p.m.
                 D ,,   ,,   ,,   ,,   2.6 p.m.
                 H.Q. ,,   ,,   ,,   ,,   2.8 p.m.

Drums to march with coys in turn.

(2) BILLETS. The following party will not visit E Johnson men at once wear by 'B' Coy. Billet LO. is noon + proceed to TAVERNELLE to take over tents for Coys — 1 N.C.O. per Coy + 1 N.C.O. for H.Q.

(3) BLANKETS. Blankets will be rolled in bundles of 10 the at Coy H.Q. ready for collection at 8 a.m. Officers kits to be ready at Coy H.Q. by 11 a.m. — Mess kits by 12.15 p.m.

(4) Headquarters will join their Coys before marching off + other details will join Coys ready for entraining. H.Q. will be divided for the 2 trains before moving off.
Fd Punishment prisoners will join their Coys.

(5) PROTECTION FROM HOSTILE AIRCRAFT as usual 'B' + 'D' Coys will find nearer L.G.s Nos 1 + 2 of team to march with transport.

(6) Officers will take steel helmets, box respirators, + full equipment + personal requirements.

(7) Men of 'B' Coy travelling on 1st train will be attached to 'A' Coy for rations + those of 'D' Coy to 'C' Coy + vice versa for 2nd train. C.Q.M.Sgts will obtain numbers before entraining.

(8) Officers train kits, 1 press box per train, + officers surplus kits (which must be clearly marked with name, Coy + Regiment of owner) to be ready for collection at 11 a.m.

ACKNOWLEDGE
                                H. Draper, Lieut + Adjt.
                                1st Battalion The Bedfordshire Regt

Copies to 1 15th Infy Bde   8 Q.M. + T.O.
           2 C.O.   9 R.S.M.
           3 H.Q. Officers   10 File
           4 O.C. A Coy   11
           5 O.C. B Coy   12 War Diary
           6 O.C. C Coy
           7 O.C. D Coy

Operation Order. No. 135.
1st Bn. Bedfordshire Regiment :   April 9th 1918.

1. The Battalion will move to SOMBRIN to-morrow 10th inst.
Bn. starting point Quartermasters Stores. —
Order of March. —   H.Q. to pass starting point at   6.50 a.m.
                    D. Coy.   6.52
                    B. Coy.   6.54
                    C. Coy.   6.56
                    A. Coy.   6.58
                    Transport   7. 0

Brigade Starting point — Cross roads formed by the FREVENT-
DOULLENS road & the NEUVILLETTE - BOUQUEMAISON road, 150 yards
west of BOUQUEMAISON Church. — Following intervals will be
observed after passing Bde Starting point. — 100 yards between Coys.
300 yards between Battalions. 100 yards between Groups of three
transport vehicles.

2. BILLETING. The following party will parade at Bn. H.Qrs.
at 6. a.m. Sgt. Sale will arrange bicycles for parties, to be at
Bn. Hd Qrs. — Capt. J. Hague, Coy. Q.M. Sgts & L/Cpl Bear. for.
H.Q. & Transport. Capt HAGUE will report to Town Major
SOMBRIN. at 8. a.m. —

3. BLANKETS. Blankets will be rolled in bundles of 10. & be
taken to Q.M. Stores by 5.30. a.m. Officers Kits, Mess Kits,
& Cooks kits will be at Coy. H.Qrs, ready for collection at
5.30. a.m.

4. PROTECTION. against HOSTILE AIRCRAFT.
As usual. — A. & C. Coys will find reserve L. G. & No 142.
for protection of transport. They will report to T.O. by
6.20. a.m.

                                    S.H. ————
                                    Lt. & a/Adjt
                                    1st Bn. Bedfordshire Regt.

SECRET.   OPERATION ORDER No. 137.   App 4   Copy No.

1st. Battalion The Bedfordshire Regiment.
April 16th. 1918.

1. 15th. Brigade is relieving 95th. Brigade to-night.
2. 1st. Bedfordshire Regiment will relieve 3 Coy's. of Gloucesters in Reserve in K.7. a and b.   "B", "C" and "D" Coy's. will relieve opposite numbers.   "A" Coy. will dig in, in K.7.a. as indicated.
3. ROUTE for all Companies :-
   Up Main drive through wood to J.23.b.3.9. - FORESTERS HOUSE - LA RUE des MORTS.
4. Companies will leave their present lines at 5 p.m. in following order :-
       "D" Coy.
       "B" "
       "C" "
       "A" "
   50 yards interval between platoons.
5. Lewis Gun limbers will convey blankets at once - on return, they will be loaded up with Lewis Guns, etc., and march up with their Companies. Also S.A.A. limbers and Pack animals.
   All S.A.A. will be dumped at new Battalion Headquarters. Transport will return to TANNAY, refill with S.A.A. at once, and await orders from Staff Captain.
6. RECONNAISANCE. On completion of relief, O.C. Coy's. will send up one Officer per Coy. 1 N.C.O. per platoon and three runners per Coy. to reconnoitre all routes to Front line Companies of Battalions in the line.
   Battalions will be disposed as under :-
       Norfolks on Right Front.
       Cheshires on Left Front.
       Warwicks in Support.
   This reconnaisance must be carried out as soon as it is dark enough.

                         O. Beale
                         Captain aid Adjt.
     1st. Battalion The Bedfordshire Regiment.

Copies to all concerned.

Copies to :-
- PILLOW.   R.S.M.
- M.T. C.O.   File.
- O.C. "A" Coy.   War Diary.
- "   "B" "
- "   "C" "
- "   "D" "
- T.O.
- Q.M.

SECRET.   Copy No.

OPERATION ORDER No. 138.

1st. Battalion The Bedfordshire Regiment.
April 20th. 1918.

1. The Battalion will relieve the Norfolk Regiment in Right Sub-sector of Brigade Sector on night 21st./22nd. April as under :-
   "A" Coy. will relieve "A" Coy. Norfolks, Right Front.
   "C" "   "   "C" "   "   Centre Front.
   "D" "   "   "D" "   "   Left Front.
   "B" "   "   "B" "   "   Immediate Support.

2. Battalion Boundaries :-
   Right. Road K.15.c.7.1. inclusive.
   Left. Road K.15.b.2.9. inclusive.

3. GUIDES. Guides of Norfolk Regiment on 21st/22nd. will meet Companies at Headquarters Norfolk Regiment, One for Coy. H.q. One per platoon.

   Companies will proceed in following order :-
   "D" Coy. via Main Road.
   "A" "   "   "   "
   "C" Coy. via ride through K.7.d. central.
   "B" "   "   "   "   "

   Headquarters will proceed independently, under Lieut S.H.Draper.

4. RECONNAISANCE Party of One Officer per Coy. and One N.C.O. per platoon will report Headquarters Norfolk Regiment at 9 p.m. to-night. They will then proceed to their respective Coy. Fronts where they will remain until their Companies arrive the following night. They will take over all dispositions, forward posts, etc., also Work, Tools, V.P.A., S.O.S., and S.A.A.

5. WATER can be obtained in any houses in the vicinity. Solidified alcohol will be issued by Quartermaster. Coy. arrangements for cooking should be made if possible.

6. All Tools in present lines will be handed over to forward party of 1st. Cheshire Regiment.
   Blankets will be rolled in bundles of ten by 2 p.m. to-morrow. T.O. will arrange to convey same back to Transport lines, where they will be cleaned and ironed by Quartermaster.

7. REPORTS. (a) Situation reports will reach Battalion Headquarters at following times :-
   4 a.m., 10 a.m., and 4 p.m.
   (b) Intelligence - at 7.30 a.m.
   (c) Casualties - 12 noon.

8. Actual time of relief will be notified later.

9. Relief complete will be reported by Runner.

                                            D. Beale
                                            Captain & Adjt.
                                    1st. Battalion The Bedfordshire Regiment.

Copies to :-
   PILLOW.   I.M.
   POINTER.   T.O.
   C.O.   R.S.M.
   O.C. "A" Coy.   File.
    "   "B" "   War Diary.
    "   "C" "
    "   "D" "

To
Headquarters,
    15th. Infantry Brigade.

Reference proposed minor operation.

1. **INFORMATION**, regarding relative positions.
    Our Front line runs from Railway at K.20.b.7.5. to K.20.b.9.9. to K.c.2.0. to K.15.c.3.1. to MERVILLE - LEMOTTE Road at K.15.c.6.1. This at present is held by a line of detached posts.
    Enemy line opposite this portion of our front as far as can be judged by Aeroplane photos runs from Railway K.21.c.15.95 to Road K.21.a.55.25. thence to Main Road K.21.a.90.80. There is also a switch trench at K.21.a.00.20. to house at K.21.a.35.50.
    There is also an advanced trench shewn very faintly from enclosure at K.21.a.50.80. to Road at K.21.a.60.100.
    The result of patrols up to the present have been to shew that the enemy only occupies the forward part of his line with very small numbers. The trench from K.21.a.50.80. was very shallow and unoccupied.
    It has not yet been established how, and in what strength the enemy is holding his line rear of the South Eastern Edge of the enclosure. It is hoped that more detailed information will be available shortly, and the appreciation is based that he has only a small forward post in the enclosure at K.21.a.

2. **OBJECT.**
    To advance our line and clear group of house and enclosure in K.21.a. of the enemy.

3. **NATURAL FEATURES.**
    The dominating natural feature is the wooded enclosure at K.21.a. the Road running through K.21.a. and thick line of hedges that surround LES LAURIERS, K.14.d.100.10.

4. **METHODS OF ATTACK.**
    These would seem to be :-
       (i) An attack with assistance of Artillery and M.G. barrages, or -
       (ii) A surprise advance at night.

5. **POSSIBLE ENEMY ACTION.**
    In the event of the first method, he would see the extent of the operation and be able to concentrate his fire on the troops, either whilst advancing or consolidating. His S.O.S. would most probably be sent up, and the battle front being always of rather a sensitive nature, it might happen that casualties would be incurred unnecessarily amongst other troops and our own supports.
       (i) If the enemy under a cover of a big barrage chose to counter attack, the possibility of him penetrating into our former front line, which is only about 70 yards from nearest edge of the enclosure, might have to be brought into consideration.
       (ii) In event of second methos being employed, it might be some time before the enemy that anything more than a large patrol action was taking place, and it is unlikely that the enemy Artillery would be able to be directed on to the place where troops are consolidating for some time.

6. **ACTION PROPOSED.**
    Assuming that only one Coy. is required to take part in the advance, and that from the Railway onwards would be the duty of other troops, the following methos is proposed :-
        There would be one Officer and 6 Other Ranks who by the result of previous patrolling would have good knowledge of nature of ground in the enclosure.
        One Platoon under this Officer would be sent forward in three parties to clear the enclosure and the house, and eventually consolidate on the far side (S.E.) of the enclosure, with forward posts pushed out as near as possible to main German line.
        The two flank platoons would similarly after allowing the first

platoon three minutes, advance on either side of the enclosure, with
a forward party well forward as in the centre platoon, and the whole
would consolidate on a line about X K.21.a.05.10. - South Eastern
edge, and along bottom edge of enclosure, thence to our old front line
posts K.21.a.60.100.

It would be necessary for a certain amount of harassing Artillery
fire on known M.G. emplacements to take place at same time as operation.
Also the enemy trench system and any tracks leading from his support
to his front line might receive a certain amount of attention at
the same time.

Previous to the operation, it would be necessary to deal with
houses on the Road running through K.21.a. from K.21.a.6.0. to
K.21.a.4.5.

The support Coy. would find the garrison for our original jumping
off position.

Rough Sketch attached.

O. Beale

Major.

23/4/18.   Commanding 1st. Battalion Bedfordshire Regt.

SECRET.   O P E R A T I O N   O R D E R   No. 139.   Copy No.

1st. Battalion Bedfordshire Regiment.
Map Ref. 36a. N.E. 1/10,000.
April 25th. 1918.

1. "A" Coy. and one platoon of "B" Coy. will advance its line from LES LAURIERS to a line running from K.21.a.05.15. to K.21.a.50.95. Road, taking in farm about K.21.a.4.6. (BEDFORD FARM) The Gloucester Regt. will conform with a similar movement on our right as far as VERTBOIS.

2. ARTILLERY will form a creeping barrage from K.20.b.7.6. to K.21.a.40.95. Rate of advance will be 1½ minutes for the first 300 yards. The barrage will stop on line of new enemy trench from about K.21.b.1.8. to K.21.c.1.9. One Newton will fire on certain targets.
Four light Trench Mortars will give a hurricane bombardment from ZERO to ZERO plus1½ minutes playing on area around BEDFORD FARM. They will then lift, and play for half an hour round building and orchard on Road around K.21.a. and M c. They will then stand to for S.O.S.

3. MACHINE GUNS (a) Two guns will fire from Zero onwards while the Artillery barrage lasts from K.15.d.4.5. on a line through K.21.a.60.05. Rate of Fire, - Intense for ten minutes, and harassing rate until Artillery barrage ceases.
(b) One M.G. will fire from K.20.b.5.8. straight down the Railway from Zero to Zerp plus10.
(c) Two M.G's. at about K.14.d.100.20. will be in readiness to move forward to BEDFORD FARM ant time afterZero.

4. ASSEMBLY. "A" Coy. will be assembles ready for the attack at 15 minutes before zero, between Eastern edge of Chateau grounds and MERVILLE - LA MOTTE Road at K.15.c.15.15 as marked out with O.C. "A" Coy. on "X" night.
One platoon of "B" Coy, commanded by 2/Lieut. F.H.Fox will form up in rear of last wave of "A" Coy. and be in reserve.
As soon as troops have moved forward, one platoon of "B" Coy. under 2/Lieut. A.E.Peel, will occupy old front line from Railway K.20.b.8.5. to Road K.15.c.80.05.
O.C. "C" Coy. will extend his right and occupy the line as far as the Road at K.15.c.80.05. vacated by "A" Coy.

5. ATTACK. At Zero, "A" Coy. will move forward to the attack, No. 2 platoon leading, followed by No. 1 and No. 3 platoons in two lines, 50 yards in rear.
   One platoon of "B" Coy. under 2/Lieut. F.H.Fox will advance 100 yards in rear of "A" Coy. and must be ready to re-inforce the attack, at any moment or assist in mopping up.
No. 2 platoon of "A" Coy. will advance with patrols on flanks of enclosure.
N.B. Barrage must be closely followed by these patrols.

6. CONSOLIDATION. The main line of resistance will be along the hedge running from K.21.a.3.5. to K.21.a.5.7. Two posts will also be dug about K.21.a.2.5. and K.21.a.05.15. to join up Railway.
Two posts will also be dug towards the MERVILLE Road to join up with the post at K.15.c.80.05.
Forward group will be pushed forward to cover the consolidation. These will be withdrawn at dawn.
The platoon of "B" Coy. will dig an immediate support approximately about 100 yards in rear of "A" Coy. in the enclosure.

7. EQUIPMENT. (i) Packs will be dumped in present positions.
(ii) Fighting kit with two bandoliers of S.A.A. will be worn - haversacks containing rations on back.
(iii) Every man will carry a pick or shovel - 10 shovels to one pick.
(iv) One bomb and one rifle grenade per man will be carried.
(v) Rations for the 26th. inst. and emergency rations will be carried.
(vi) Waterbottles to be full.
(vii) One round of white V.P.A. per man will be carried, and three sets of S.O.S. Signals per platoon, (GREEN 1")
(viii) Every Officer will carry two rounds of RED V.P.A. 1".
N.B. O.C. Coy. will send up one RED Rocket on objective being gained.

8. COMMUNICATIONS. (i) Signalling Officer will arrange for telephone and lamp to go forward with "A" Coy.
9. Forward Battalion Headquarters will be established at LES LAURIERS at 3 p.m. 25th. April, where all reports will be sent.
   If a barrage is heavy, on LESLAURIERS, reports can be sent via "C" Coy's. H.Q.
10. Zero hour will be about 9 p.m. 25th. inst. exact hour will be notified later
11. Watches will be synchronised by Runner about 4 p.m. and before 7 p.m.
12. MEDICAL. Dressing Station will remain at same place where walking wounded should proceed. There will be a bearer squad at LES LAURIERS to deal with stretchercases.
13. R.S.M. will report to Adjutant to receive instructions re stragglers post.
14. Prisoners to be sent direct to old Battalion Headquarters. Support platoon of "B" Coy. will provide escort. On no account are men of "A" Coy to be sent back with prisoners.

ACKNOWLEDGE.

                                                  Capt. & Adjt.
                  1st. Bn. Bedfordshire Regiment.

Copies to :-
    H.Q. 15th. Infy. Bde.
    O.C. "A" Coy.
     "   "B" "
     "   "C" "
     "   "D" "
    O.C., 12th. GloucesterRegt.
    C.O.
    O.C. M.G.C.
    O.C., T.M.B.
    File.
    War Diary.

To
PILLOW.

Report on attack and taking of enclosure at K.21.a.
Reference attached sketch map.

1. ASSEMBLY. "A" Coy. 1st. Bedf. Regt. and one platoon of "B" Coy. assembled for the attack at 9.15 p.m. according to plan. The barrage opened to time, some guns were firing short – 18 pounder shrapnel. About 12 casualties were caused by this including O.C. "A" Coy. (Capt. F.Hague) who however went forward with his Coy.

2. THE ATTACK, was carried out according to plan. Two sections of the support platoon "B" Coy. had to be sent forward to the right platoon to replace casualties. This right platoon suffered more heavily than the remainder of the Coy.
Ten unwounded prisoners and one wounded prisoner were brought in, also one M.G.
The RED Rocket, (signal for gaining objective) was first seen at 9.38 p.m. and again at 9.58 p.m.
At 10.35 p.m. message was received by Runner from O.C. "A" Coy. saying all objectives had been taken. At 11 p.m. Capt. F.Hague reported that he had been all round his line and that he was in touch with the Gloucester Regt. on his right, and "C" Coy. 1st. Bedf. R. on his left. He then came to Battalion H.Q. at LES LAURIERS, where it was discovered that he had a bad wound in the thigh. He was sent down to the Dressing Station at 11.30 p.m. Telephonic communication was obtained with Front line at 11 p.m.

3. CONSOLIDATION. "A" Coy. are holding the line of the objective as laid down in Brigade O.O. and have dug in, in accordance with attached sketch map.
At 10.15 p.m. 2 Bde. M.G's were sent up, and took up positions in right and left corners of wood as indicated.
The house at K.21.a.4.5. has been cleared and is being held at night. This house is about 50 yards in front of (i.e. S.E.) of bottom right hand corner of enclosure.
The line is at present held as per attached sketch map.

Our estimated casualties are 25 wounded including Capt. F.Hague, and killed at present unknown, though believed not heavy. – probably about 15.
The front line has been visited, and the trenches are well sited. One M.G. has been captured.

Time – 1.30 a.m.
April 26th. 1918.

O Beale Capt & Major.
Commanding 1st. Bedfordshire Regt.

SECRET.
Copy No.

OPERATION ORDER No. 140.

1st. Battalion Bedfordshire Regiment.
Map Ref. 36a. N.E. 1/20,000.

April 26th. 1918.

1. Battalion will be relieved on the night of the 26th/27th. as under :-
   Right Coy. "A". From K.21.a.15.05. to Road K.21.a.80.90. exclusive, to be relieved by a Coy. of the D.C.L.I.
   Centre Coy. "C". From Road K.21.a.80.90. inclusive to Canal at K.15.d.2.8. by a Coy. of the K.O.S.B. "D" Coy.
   Left Coy. "D" Coy. From Canal to corner of emclosure K.15.b.1.9. by a Coy. of the K.O.S.B. "B" Coy.
   Support Coy. "B". at K.15.c. central. will be relieved by a Coy. of the K.O.S.B. ("A" Coy.)
   2/Lieut. V.E.Farr will hand over all these trenches to this Coy. of K.O.S.B. They will not relieve the two platoons of "B" Coy. in Front of LES LAURIES.

2. RECONNAISANCE. One Officer per Coy. and One N.C.O. per platoon of D.C.L.I. and K.O.S.B. will report at Battalion Headquarters at 8.30 p.m. whence they will be guided to their respective Coy Fronts, and stay there the night 26/27th.

3. GUIDES. on scale of One O.R. per platoon, and one O.R. for H.Q. (Coy) will meet relieving Units at Bn. H.Q. (Faggot Stack) at 8.45 p.m. on the 27th. inst. Guides will report to the Intelligence Officer. They will each be in possession of a slip of paper shewing which platoon and Coy. of relieving Unit they are to guide.
   Two guides from 2/Lieut. Farr's platoon "B" Coy. will be sufficient for support Coy.

4. ALL WORK in progress and proposed, all trench stores, S.O.S. rockets, V.P.A., etc., will be handed over, also tools. The two extra bandoliers per man will be collected in platoon or section dumps and kept dry and handed over. Lists of all trench stores etc., to be handed over will be sent to Battalion Headquarters by daybreak 27/4/18 by runner.

5. The greatest care must be taken in handing over forward posts, so that no ground is lost.

6. On completion of relief Coy's. will withdraw by complete platoons to bivouacs at J.20.b. Q.M. will arrange for one guide per platoon and one for Coy. H.Q., and two for Battalion Headquarters to be at Battalion Headquarters by 10.30 p.m. to guide Coy's. back to bivouacs.

7. T.O. will arrange for limbers to collect spare Lewis Gun Magazines at Bn. H.Q. also Lewis Guns and magazines of Coy's. Sgt. Faulder will supervise loading.

8. RELIEF COMPLETE will be reported by wire using following code message :-
   "BARBEDWWIRE".
   O.C. Coy's. will also report at Bn. H.Q., on their way out.

ACKNOWLEDGE.

O Beale Capt
Capt. & Adjt.

Copies to :-
Bde. H.Q.   Intell. Off.
D.C.L.I.   T.O. and Rear H.Q.
K.O.S.B.   Q.M.
C.O.   File.
O.C. "A" Coy.   R.S.M.
    " "B" "   War Diary.
    " "C" "
    " "D" "

To:-
Headquarters,
    15th. Infantry Brigade.

    The enemy attacked our right Coy. this morning at about 4.30 a.m. behind a heavy barrage. About 200 enemy advanced to within 100 yards under cover of their barrage and the mist. Our M.G., L.G., and rifle fire broke up the attack.
    The S.O.S. was not sent up on our front.
    It is reported that we are still in touch with the 12th. Gloucester Regt.
    The Coy. has had about 15 casualties, caused by shell fire. Capt. W.W. White, Commanding this Coy. front line has been wounded.

Time - 7.48 a.m.

27/4/18.

S. Beale
Capt. & Adjt.
1st. Bn. Bedfordshire Regiment.

N. YELLOW.

The following is a continuation of report about the enemy counter attack in the early morning of the 27th. April 1918 :-

The barrage was put down chiefly on our part of the line, running through enclosure and going up thence to the 12th. Gloucesters.

There is no doubt that the enemy suffered considerable casualties.

Opposite the centre of our line, some of the enemy were seen to throw away their arms and equipment, and turn tail. Our Lewis Gun on the right, which was at K.21.a.05.15, was enabled to enfilade the attack, and greatly assisted.

Touch was maintained during the action with the 12th. Gloucesters.

Our patrols which were out on the night of the 27th. to cover the relief, report finding number of enemy dead.

28/4/18.

Major.

Commanding P U G .

1st Bedfordshire Regt

May 1918

VOLUME No.

BRITISH SALONIKA FORCE

WAR DIARY.

VOL. No.	UNIT	PERIOD FROM	TO
6.	320 Siege Batty. R.G.A.	1.10.18	31.10.18
6.	322 do.	"	"
11.	424 do.	"	"
6.	445 Siege Batty. R.G.A.	1.10.18	31.10.18
20.	810 M.T. Coy. A.S.C.	1.10.18	31.10.18
6.	1031 do.	"	"
6.	1032 do.	"	"
6.	1083 M.T. Coy. A.S.C.	1.10.18	31.10.18

CONFIDENTIAL.

WAR DIARY

OF

1st Bedfordshire Regt.

for the month of

May 1918.

E.G.? ?
Lt. Col.
Commanding

Army Form C. 2118.

WAR DIARY
or
INTELLIGENCE SUMMARY
(Erase heading not required.)

Instructions regarding War Diaries and Intelligence Summaries are contained in F.S. Regs., Part II. and the Staff Manual respectively. Title Pages will be prepared in manuscript.

Place	Date	Hour	Summary of Events and Information	Remarks and references to Appendices
MAY	1st		Battalion in support in NIEPPE FOREST. Headquarters at L'EPPINETTE	
	2nd		As above	
	3rd		Battalion moved up to support position relieving 19/Worcesters. Regiment party of 2 officers & 128 other ranks. Surplus Personnel, moved back to TANNAY. See A.F.391 attached	APP I
	4th		As above. Battalion employed making tracks to front line trenches. Headquarters, carrying parties, digging, wiring support line.	
	5th		As above. Casualties 1 killed & 4 O.Rs wounded	
	6th		As above	
	7th		As above. 1 O.R. wounded	
	8th		As above	
	9th		Battalion relieved 1st Battalion Cheshire Regt in front line, left sector. Nidd Post. Casualties: 6 O.Rs wounded. See O.O. 141	APP II

WAR DIARY or INTELLIGENCE SUMMARY

Army Form C. 2118.

Place	Date	Hour	Summary of Events and Information	Remarks and references to Appendices
	10th		As above. Enemy machine guns very active	
	11th		As above. Casualties 3 ORs wounded	
	12th		As above. Casualties 6 ORs wounded	
	13th		As above. Casualties 3 ORs killed	
	14th / 15th		As above. Work with Battalion was on front line carrying on in improving trenches, making front line continuous & wiring the whole front. A new trench was dug by the right Company to support Platoon. R.E.s put in 2 new Bty Stephens Shelters in Right Support Company' Headquarters Battalion Headquarters worked on existing Hutt Houses & new ones built.	
	16th		As above. At 9h Regt & 10th Welch Battalion relieved by 14th Battalion Royal Warwickshire Regiment & withdrew to VILLERS Camp.	APP III

Wd 142

Army Form C. 2118.

WAR DIARY
or
INTELLIGENCE SUMMARY
(Erase heading not required.)

Instructions regarding War Diaries and Intelligence Summaries are contained in F. S. Regs., Part II. and the Staff Manual respectively. Title Pages will be prepared in manuscript.

Place	Date	Hour	Summary of Events and Information	Remarks and references to Appendices
	17th		In Camp as above. Battalion employed cleaning up, changing khaki etc.	
	18th		As above. Battalion employed on Divisional Line. 2 Coys 9pm to 1am. 2 Coys 1pm to 4pm.	
	19th		In Camp as above, work on Divisional Line as above. Battalion relieved by 1st Battalion the Norfolk Regiment, at night, such them 2 Companies & Headquarters to TANNAY, 2 Companies to THIENNES.	
	20th		In Billets as above, 5.30 a.m. "Tent Alarm" sounded & Battalion proceeded by light railway to take up battle positions, working parties found at THIENNES station etc.	
	21st		Battalion on contact aeroplane scheme, took up positions at 4 P.M. closed at 10 P.M. Proceeded by companies to the Baths.	
	22nd		As above. Battalion found parties to work on Divisional Line, moved up to SPRESIANO Camp at night relieved 1st Battalion the Cheshire Regt.	

WAR DIARY or INTELLIGENCE SUMMARY

Army Form C. 2118.

(Erase heading not required.)

Place	Date	Hour	Summary of Events and Information	Remarks and references to Appendices
	23rd		In Camp as above, training carried on under company arrangements	
	24th		In Camp as above. Half Bn. "S" No forced training carried on under Company arrangements. Working party found for Brigade R.E.	
	25th		As above. Training, working party only, as above	
	26th		As above	
	27th		As above	
	28th		Party proceeded to front line at night to take over ready for relief next day, casualties 2 O.R.s wounded.	
	29th		As above. Battalion preparing to move to front line. 9 p.m. Battalion moved up & relieved Battalion the King's Regiment. See C.O. #3 in front line	App IV
	30th		As above. Enemy shelled considerably with gas shell casualties 1 O.R. wounded	
	31st		In line as above. Enemy artillery active in some sectors. Casualties nil.	

Capt. E.C. Hestell 9.3 Bn. Worcester
J. Marshall
Lt. Bn. C.O.
(Bn. adjutant)

1 Bedpost Regt
Vol 43

WARNING ORDER. A327 APPI

1. On the night of the 3rd/4th. the Battalion will relieve the 1st. Bn. East Surreys in support. Headquarters at XXXXXXXXXX J.24.d.6.4.

2. Reconnasaince party consisting of One Officer and one runner per per Coy. and one N.C.O. per platoon will proceed to the line to-day, and take over from their opposite letter Companies.
These parties will remain with the East Surreys until relieved by Battalion on the following day.

3. Intelligence Officer and 2 Runners from Battalion Headquarters will accompany this party.

4. Parties will report to the Headquarters of the East Surreys at 6 p.m. to-night.

2/8/18.

P. Beale
Pug.
Capt. & Adjt.

APP II

SECRET.

OPERATION ORDER No. 141.

Copy No.

1st. Battalion The Bedfordshire Regiment.

May 8th. 1918.

1. Battalion will relieve the Cheshire Regiment in the left sub-sector to-morrow, May 9th/10th. as under :-

	Bedfords.	Cheshires.	Move off from present position at	Route.
Left Front.	"B" Coy.	"C" Coy.		via "D" Coy. line - Railway K.14.d.15.40.
Centre.	"D" "	"B" "		Same route as "C" Coy.
Right.	"C" "	"D" "		Main track K.13.d.8.2. to enclosure K.20.c.
Support.	"A" "	"A" "		via Railway K.14.d.15.40.
	H.Q.	H.Q.	8.45 p.m.	via Wired track.

2. **GUIDES** of Cheshires, one per platoon will meet Companies at respective front line at H.Q.

3. **PATROLS.** Strong standing patrols will at once be sent out as close to the enemy as possible. These patrols will be posted by an Officer and will **NOT** withdraw until daybreak.
   NOTE. - Our S.O.S. barrage is 300 yards front of our front line.

4. **STAND TO.** As it is the first night in a new sector, no Officers or men will sleep until after stand down in the morning.

5. **RATIONS** For "B", "D" and "A" Coy's. rations will be brought on pack animals as far as ration dump on Railway K.14.d.15.40. These Companies will each send 3 men to draw rations, water and half tea from this dump - not more than three men per Coy. are to be away at the same time. Fighting order to be worn.
   For "C" Coy. rations etc., will go as far as Coy. H.Q. Rations should be at at the above dumps about 9.30 p.m. These dumps must be well reconnoitred to-night.

6. Fighting order, plus Great Coats rolled, waterproof sheets and Mess Tins.
DRESS. Packs will be dumped near light railway to-morrow by 2 p.m. Q.M. will arrange for the Drums to be at Battalion Headquarters at this time. They will fetch the packs of Coy's. down to Railway on main diagonal road and will see them loaded in the train, and taken back to Transport. T.O. will arrange for accommodation on train. Packs must be clearly marked with the Regimental Number, Name and Coy.
BLANKETS will be ready same time and proceed by same means. No surplus kit of any kind is to taken to the front line.

7. **STORES.** All stores, work etc., and explosives and S.O.S. are to be taken over. One N.C.O. and one runner in addition to reconnoitring parties already detailed, will proceed to front line to take over, and remain there until their Coy's. arrive there to-morrow night.

8. **TIME** will be sent round Coy's. to-morrow at 4 p.m. Relief complete to be reported by wire, using the names of C.S.M's. as code word. Also by Runner.
   These orders will be destroyed before proceeding to front line.

O.Beale.
(sd) Capt. & Adjt.
1. Bedfordshire Regt.

Copies to :-
Bde. H.Q.
O.C. "A" Coy.
" "B" "
" "C" "
" "D" "

T.O.
Q.M.
R.S.M.
File.
War Diary.

May 1917

May 1917

SECRET.
Copy No. 10

OPERATION ORDER No. 142.

1st Battalion The Bedfordshire Regiment.

May 15th. 1918.

1. Battalion will be relieved by TEHE on night of 16th/17th. May as follows :-
   "A" Coy. TEHE will relieve our "C" Coy.   Right Coy.
   "B" "   "   "   "   "   "D" Coy.   Centre "
   "D" "   "   "   "   "   "B" Coy.   Left   "
   "C" "   "   "   "   "   "A" "   Support "

2. All stores, S.A.A. (except 120 rounds per man) V.P.A., S.O.S., etc., will be handed over. Tools must be collected in platoon dumps. Lists of stores to be handed over must reach Battalion Headquarters at daybreak to-morrow. All work in progress, etc., and action in case of an attack must be explained to relieveing Coy's.

3. Detailed work reports with sketch map, shewing wire, posts, etc., and shewing work done during tour must reach Battn. H.Q. by daybreak to-morrow

4. GUIDES. One guide per platoon will report to I.O. at Battn. H.Q. to-night, where they will remain until relief arrives. I.O. will arrange to meet relieving Unit at K.13.b.3.6. Junction of Infantry Row and VIA ROMA at 9 p.m. Relief complete will be reported by wire using names of C.S.M's. as code, and also by runner.

5. T.O. will arrange necessary Transport for Lewis Guns, H.Q. Cooks kit, Signal and Mess Kit.

6. On completion of relief, Companies will withdraw by platoons to VILLORBA Camp, J.20.b. reporting their arrival to Capt. G. de C.Millais.

7. The Battalion will be at the disposal of the XIIIth. Brigade until further orders.

8. O.C. Coy's. will commit these orders to memory and destroy same immediately afer being read.

(sd) O.Beale,
Capt. & Adjt.
TEHE.

Acknowledge.
Issued at 9 p.m.

Copies to :-
O.C. "A" Coy.   Capt. Millais.
 "   "B" "   T.O. & Q.M.   O.C., TEHE.
 "   "C" "   R.S.M.
 "   "D" "   War Diary.

SECRET.   Copy No. 12

OPERATION ORDER No. 43.

1st. Battalion The Bedfordshire Regiment.

May 28th. 1918.

1. On the night of the 29th/30th. Battalion will relieve the 1st. Norfolks in the Right Sub-Sector. After relief, Coy's. will be disposed as follows :-
    "B" on the Right.   "D" on the left.
    "A" in the centre.   "C" in Support.

2. The following alterations were made on the night of the 26th/27th.
    Right. Coy. - No change.
    Centre Coy. - One platoon withdrawn to occupy positions immediately N. of River BOURRE in old front line K.15.a.9.2.
    Left Coy.   - One platoon withdrawn to occupy position in our old front line at K.9.d.6.3.
    Support Coy. - One platoon withdrawn from old front line to trench in rear of SURREY FARM enclosure at K.9.d.0.4.

3. ROUTE. Along VIA ROMA to the HALT, thence direct to Coy. fronts.
4. GUIDES, of 1st. Norfolk Regt. one per platoon will meet Coy's. at the HALT.
5. SKETCH Maps showing exact disposition, wire and state of trenches will be sent to Battalion Headquarters before daybreak on the morning of the 30th.
6. Party of one N.C.O. per platoon will be sent on to-night by respective Coy's. to take over stores, work, etc., This party will remain in trenches until arrival of Coy's.
7. WORK. Front line Coy's. will concentrate on wiring their respective fronts. Barricades in the form of Breastworks will be constructed at all places where Roads pass through our front line. The Road at K.9.d.8.3. is inclusive to Left Battalion.
8. Companies will leave Camp in the following order :-
    200 yards distance between platoons.
        "B", - "D", - "A", - "C", - H.Q.
    Head of column will leave Camp at 9 p.m.
9. RELIEF COMPLETE will be reported by the name of C.Q.M.Sgts. in each Coy. by wire also by Runner.

ACKNOWLEDGE.

                                                        Captain & Adjt.
                                            1st. Battalion Bedfordshire Regiment.

Copies to :-
    1. Bde. H.   7. Q.M.
    2. O.C., 1st. Norfolk Regt.   8. T.O.
    3. O.C. "A" Coy.   9. R.S.M.
    4. "   "B" "   10. File.
    5. "   "C" "   11, 12 and 13. War Diary.
    6. "   "D" "

1st "Bedfordshire Regt

June 1918

VOLUME No.

BRITISH SALONIKA FORCE

WAR DIARY.

VOL. No.	UNIT	PERIOD FROM	TO
21.	13TH Heavy Batty. R.G.A.	1.10.18	31.10.18
37.	18TH do.	"	"
30.	190TH do.	"	"

CONFIDENTIAL.

H.Q.
15th INFANTRY BDE.
No. A.24
Date. 3.7.18

Register..........
Part No..........
Volume No. 9B 44

WAR DIARY

OF

1st Bedfordshire Regt.

for the month of

June 1918.

A.M.Warner
of Staff Captain 15th Infy Bde
for G.C.
15 C
Commanding 15th Infantry Brigade.

3/7/1918.

WAR DIARY or INTELLIGENCE SUMMARY

Army Form C. 2118.

Place	Date	Hour	Summary of Events and Information	Remarks and references to Appendices
	1/6/18		Battalion in front line. 2/Lt F Hughes was wounded, 2 ORs killed & 3 wounded.	
	2/6/18		Battalion in line (front). There was considerable arv shelling but no casualties.	
	3/6/18		About 1 Lt H.J. Everett M.C. slightly wounded & OR's & 14 ORs were wounded. The enemy's made a raid on our left.	
	4/6/18		Battalion was relieved by R W Kent Regt & withdrew to billets at Steenbecque.	
	5/6/18		We had no casualties. Battalion in billets, rest & clean up.	
	6/6/18		Training under Coy arrangements. Tanks are allotted at Arcade, boarded early in afternoon owing to heavy showers.	
	7/6/18		It H Everett M.C. slightly wounded by the Battalion. Baths are allotted at Aoeuf. Polsionly. An attack scheme by the Battalion.	
	8/6/18		Promoted to 2/Lt & posted to this Battalion.	
	9/6/18		Battalion training - companies practice the attack.	
	10/6/18		Church service for all denominations. a draft of 21 ORs joined, one Lance Corporal & 20 Privates.	
	11/6/18		Battalion training under Company arrangements. The Battalion practised the attack. 1st ORs join from Rein Comp etc.	
	12/6/18		Transport holds operation order issued to support line in absence of that Bn. D. Reg in reserve. The Battalion move to support line.	App. I.
	13/6/18		Battalion in support line. Platoons were employed in improving their positions in above.	
	14/6/18		The line is shelled again. The Battalion is employed in improving their positions in above.	
	15/6/18		In front and positions are shelled by enemy. 2/Lt P R was wounded.	

Army Form C. 2118.

WAR DIARY
or
INTELLIGENCE SUMMARY
(Erase heading not required.)

Instructions regarding War Diaries and Intelligence Summaries are contained in F. S. Regs., Part II. and the Staff Manual respectively. Title Pages will be prepared in manuscript.

Place	Date	Hour	Summary of Events and Information	Remarks and references to Appendices
	13/6/18		Battalion in same position. Enemy stands active, the firing 20 rounds rapid firing to pm to 10 midnight. Grenades being thrown by P.O. a E.O. Shin D.O. took place at 2 a.m. 2 O.R.s wounded.	
	14/6/18		Battalion in same position. Pro Brigade 233 returned no enemy snipes have been reported. Coming from St Firmin 273/Lt H.J. did not return from patrol.	
	15/6/18		2/Lt W.E. joined. 2/Lt A.J. Wilkins wounded on duty the O.R. wounded.	App. II
	16/6/18		Above Enemy Stando seen No fires only me, 2nd Lt H.J. Guthrie MC returning to regiment inc. Stratton returned.	
	17/6/18		Battalion relieved by 2nd Rifle Brigade and on relief was conveyed to Rubempré. 2nd Lt D.J.S. Inspected.	
	18/6/18		Training. Every man fell out wounded by sniper. One man reported near the encampment.	
	19/6/18		Battalion temporary Brigade inspection. Fitting a P.T. 2/Lt Lowcock 2/Lt SeKeaux joined Batt. in front lines.	App. III
	20/6/18		Moved up to front line by F.E. 1 O.R. wounded. 3 Enemy Rep. Lear have joined duty. Court of Enquiry to men in duty	
	21/6/18		Bat. front out in search of Enemy L.G. but Enemy silent hit by heavy L.O.R's wounded at return.	
	22/6/18		Battalion relieved by 2nd Bn. Cheshire Regt Enemy silent. Bn. O.R.s were proceeded to Vadencourt. Were no mishap to the D.S.O. totally the wounded. Wounded wounded wounded	App. IV
	23/6/18		Br. I was allowed at Vadencourt. Cleaning up etc. 10 Officers and other ranks joined.	

Army Form C. 2118.

WAR DIARY
or
INTELLIGENCE SUMMARY
(Erase heading not required.)

Place	Date	Hour	Summary of Events and Information	Remarks and references to Appendices
	26/4/18		Training under Company arrangements. Enemy active shelling round forest & the camp.	
	27/4/18		Kingdom Lanes Battn. down Ypres Area. 1 O.R. killed, ouch R.S.M. or Recon. 2 Officers & 5 O.R's employed with the assistance teams. Company training usual. Weather quiet, rather enemy shelled camp.	
	28/4/18		C.O & the body wounded near Wieltje Camp.	
	29/4/18		3 offrs & 24 O.Rs join the Battn. Battalion trains under Company arrangements.	Apx I
	30/4/18		Battalion relieve 1st Bn Cheshire Regt in the front line.	

M. Lieutenant Major
Commanding 1st Battalion
The Bedfordshire Regt.

SECRET.   Copy No. 12

OPERATION ORDER No. 143.

1st. Battalion Bedfordshire Regiment.

June 12th. 1918.

Map – Refere nce 35.A. 1/40,000.

---

1. Battalion will relieve the 1st. Bn. D.C.L.I. in support.
2. Order of march – H.Q., "B", "C", "D" and "A" Coy's.
   5 minutes between each Coy.
   Head of H.Q. to cross pontoon bridge at B.7.c.4.5. at 2.15 p.m.
3. ROUTE – Pontoon Bridge. (B.7.c.4.5.) along canal to B.8.c.7.9. –
   Main ST. VAAST Road to 1'Epinette, from thence inside edge of wood and along VIA RMA.
4. GUIDES – Guides at the rate of one per platoon will meet Companies at the house by old Brewing Station, B.13.a.8.4.
5. O.C. Coy's. will render to Orderly Room before marching off, certificates that billets vacated by them have been left clean and free from S.A.A. and that des appliances are borrowed.
6. Administrative arrangements as in Battalion Orders dated 11/6/18.
7. Relief complete will be reported by Runner.
8. Necessary precautions will be taken in case of enemy Aircraft.

ACKNOWLEDGE.

(signed) A.B. Kirkland

Lieut. & A/Adjt.
1st. Battalion Bedford Bedfordshire Regiment.

Copies to :-
1. H.Q. 15th. Infy. Bde.
2. O.C. 1st. D.C.L.I.
3. O.C. "A" Coy.
4. " "B" "
5. " "C" "
6. " "D" "
7. Q.M.
8. T.O.
9. R.S.M.
10. File.
11.)
12.) War Diary.
13.)

SECRET.

app. II

Copy No. 13

OPERATION ORDER No. 146.

1st. Battalion The Bedfordshire Regiment.
June 18th. 1918.

1. The Battalion will relieve the 1st. Battalion Cheshire Regiment in left Sub-sector on the night 18th/19th. June.
2. **DISPOSITION.** Front line — "C" Coy. On the left —
   On   "A" Coy on the right.
   Support —   "B" Coy on the left.
               "D" Coy on the right.
   Companies will relieve as follows :—
      "C" Coy. Bedfords relieve "D" Coy Cheshires.
      "A" "   "   " "A" "   "
      "B" "   "   " "C" "   "
      "D" "   "   " "B" "   "
3. **GUIDES.** One guide per platoon and one for Coy. Headquarters will be ready to meet Companies at 10 p.m. at the following places :—
      "C" Coy. at junction of broad guage railway and support line at K.20.b.6.4.
      "A" and "D" Coy's. at end of light railway K.20.a.9.0.
      "B" Coy at point where light railway crosses main MERVILLE Road about K.14.b.3.3.
4. Companies will proceed in the following order :—
      "C", "A", "D".
   200 yards interval between platoons, five minutes between Companies.
   Head of "C" Coy. leaving Camp at 9.30 p.m.
   ROUTE — Along light railway running from K.14.c.25.60. to K.20.a.9.0.
      "B" Coy. will proceed independently along branch line from K.14.c.15.85. to K.14.b.3.3.
      Headquarters move independently at 9.15 p.m. to Cheshire H.Q. at K.13.b.9.4.
5. **RECONNAISANCE.** One Officer per Company will reconnoitre their Coy. front to-night. One N.C.O. per platoon and one for Coy. Headquarters will proceed to the line at 1 a.m. on the 18th. to take over trench stores, remaining in the line until the arrival of their Companies.
6. All mens packs and surplus Coy. kit not required in the line will be dumped at the junction of light railway and VIA ROMA, (K.13.a.7.5.) by 7.30 p.m. One man per Coy. will look after this kit until the arrival of the ration train, when it will be handed over to Coy. Q.M.Sgts.
7. **RATIONS.** Rations will be issued before the Battalion moves off, each man carrying his own rations up to the line.
8. List of stores taken over to reach Battalion Headquarters before dawn.
9. Completion of relief will be reported by name of C.S.M., by wire and confirmed by runner.

ACKNOWLEDGE.

(sd) A.H.O.Riddell.   Lieut. & A/Adjt.
1st. Battalion Bedfordshire Regiment.

Copies to :—
1. Bde. Headquarters.   7. T.O.
2. O.C. 1st. Cheshires.   8. Q.M.
3. O.C. "A" Coy.   9. R.S.M.
4. "   "B" "   10. File.
5. "   "C" "   11.)
6. "   "D" "   12.) War Diary.
                              13.)

SECRET.   Copy No. 11

OPERATION ORDER No. 147.

1st. Battalion Bedfordshire Regiment.

Date. 21/6/18.

1. The Battalion frontage will be shortened on the night of the 21st/22nd. from the present position on the right to the MERVILLE - LA MOTTE Road exclusive at K.21.a.99.90.
This readjustment will take place in both front line and support south of the MERVILLE Road.

2. The disposition of the Battalion will then be as follws :-
   Front line.   "A" Coy. from their present position on the right at VERTBOIS to the junction of the C.T. and fire trench at K.20.d.7.9.
   "C" Coy. from K.20.d.7.9. to the MERVILLE - LA MOTTE Road.
   "C" Coy's. H.Q. will move to Slit trench at K.21.a.15.45
   "A" Coy's. H.Q. remaining in present position.

   Support line.   "D" Coy from their present position on the right to point where support line crosses stream at K.20.d.25.95.
   "B" Coy. from the stream at K.20.d. 25.95. to the MERVILLE - LA MOTTE Road.
   "D" Coy's. H.Q. will remain in present position.
   "B" Coy's. H.Q. will move to Slit trench at K.20.b.45.50

3. Details of guides, time etc., will be arranged between Coy. Commanders concerned in both Battalions.

4. Coy. Commanders will arrange to reconnoitre their new area.

5. A sketch map shewing position of Lewis Guns and Platoons to be sent to Battalion Headquarters as soon as possible after completion of re-adjustments.

6. Completion of readjustment of line will reported by the names of C.S.M's. by wire and also by runner.

ACKNOWLEDGE.

                                    (sd) W.H.L.Barnett,   Capt for O.C.
                            1st. Battalion Bedfordshire Regiment.

Copies to :-
1. Bde. H.Q.
2. O.C. 1st. D.C.L.I.   7. I.O.
3. O.C. "A" Coy.   8. File.
4. "   "B" "   9.)
5. "   "C" "   10.) War Diary.
6. "   "D" "   11.)

SECRET.   App IV   Copy No. 10

OPERATION ORDER No. 148.

1st. Battalion The Bedfordshire Regiment.
Ref. Map France 56.A. N.E. 1/20,000. Ed.7.   June 23rd. 1918.

1. The Battalion will be relieved by the 1st. Bn. Cheshire Regt. on the night 24th./25th. June 1918.
2. On relief Companies will proceed by platoons into Brigade Reserve at VILLORBA Camp at J.15.d.
3. ROUTE – Along light railway from K.20.a.9.0. to K.13.b.7.9. and then along VIA ROMA and ROTTEN ROW to l'Epinette, where they will be met by guides.
4. GUIDES – Companies will provide guides at the rate of one per platoon, and one for Coy. Headquarters to guide the incoming unit, to be K.20.a.9.0 and 10.30 p.m.
5. All trench stores, defence schemes, aeroplane photographs and work in progress will be handed over and receipt obtained by Coy's.
6. Machine Gun Limbers will meet the Companies at K.13.b.7.9.
7. T.O. will arrange to have Officers kits, Cookers etc., taken to VILLORBA Camp.
8. Instructions regarding Cooks utensils, Signallers kit, etc., will be issued later.
9. Q.M. will arrange to take over huts at VILLORBA Camp to-morrow morning, and see that guides are at l'Epinette at 11.30 p.m. to guide platoons in.
10. Q.M. will arrange for a hot meal to be given to the troops on arrival at VILLORBA Camp.
11. Completion of relief to be reported by the word "STRAFE". by wire and also by runner.

On arrival at billets, Coy's. will report present to Battalion H.Q.

ACKNOWLEDGE.   (sd) A.H.O.Riddell. Lt. & A/Adj.
                                1st. Bn. Bedfordshire Regiment.

Copies to :-
1. Bde. H.Q.
2. O.C. 1st. Cheshires
3. O.C. "A" Coy.
4. "   "B" "
5. "   "C" "
6. "   "D" "
7. Q.M. and T.O.
8. R.S.M.
9. File.
10.)
11.) War Diary.
12.)

SECRET.   Copy No. 10.
OPERATION ORDER No. 142.

1st. Battalion The Bedfordshire Regiment.
Ref: Map, France 36.A. N.E. 1/20,000. Ed. 7.
                                               June 30th. 1918.
_____

Battalion will relieve the 1st. Battalion The Cheshire Regiment in the left sub-sector of the LE BART sector of the front on the night of the 30th. June and 1st. July, 1918.

DISPOSITION.   "B" Coy. - Left front line.   "D" Coy - Right front line.
                  "C" Coy. - Left support.   "A" Coy. - Right support

Companies will move off in the following order :-
        "D", "B", "C", and "A".
100 yards between platoons, and five minutes between Companies. Head of "D" Coy. leaving Camp at 6 p.m.

ROUTE AND TIMING.   Will be notified later.

All pack packs, Officers valises, and surplus kit not wanted by the line will be collected at the entrance to Camp, by 5 p.m.
Mess Boxes and Officers kits for the line will be at the same place by 8 p.m. One servant per Coy. will accompany these.

LIMBERS. Limbers will take the load as far as I.K.13.b.45.30, where they will be unloaded, and picked up by Companies as they pass.
One N.C.O. per Coy. will proceed with these limbers.

RATIONS. Rations will be issued before moving off. Hot tea will be issued during the night. Time to be notified later.

LINE OF MARCH. Taken over will reach orderly Room by 6 a.m.

COMPLETION. of relief will be reported by the word "VIMMY", both by wire and runner.

                                                W.K.L.Barnett Maj
ACKNOWLEDGE.   for Lieut. & A/Adjt.

1st. Battalion Bedfordshire Regiment.

Copies to :-
   1. H.Q. 15th. Infy. Bde.   7. T.O. and T.M.
   2. O.C. 1st. Cheshires.   8. R.S.M.
   3. O.C. "A" Coy.   9. File.
   4. " "B" Coy.   10.)
   5. O.C. "C" Coy.   11.) War Diary.
   6. " "D" "   12.)

1st Bedfordshire Regt

July 1918

VOLUME No.

BRITISH SALONIKA FORCE

WAR DIARY.

			PERIOD
VOL. No.	UNIT	FROM	TO
25.	20th H. Batty. R.G.A.	1.10.18	31.10.18
20.	185 do.	"	"
20.	196 H. Batty. R.G.A.	1.10.18	31.10.18
25.	43rd Siege Batty "	"	"
20.	376 M.T. Coy. A.S.C.	1.10.18	31.10.18

CONFIDENTIAL.

WAR DIARY

OF

Bedfordshire Regt.

for the month of July 1918.

Register..........
Part No..........
Volume No...... Vol 45

C. M. Barnes
Commanding 15th Infantry Brigade.

31/7/1918.

Army Form C. 2118.

WAR DIARY
or
INTELLIGENCE SUMMARY

(Erase heading not required.)

Instructions regarding War Diaries and Intelligence Summaries are contained in F.S. Regs., Part II. and the Staff Manual respectively. Title Pages will be prepared in manuscript.

Place	Date	Hour	Summary of Events and Information	Remarks and references to Appendices
	JULY 1918			
	1st		Battalion releived The 1st Battalion The Cheshire Regiment.on night 30/6 1/7 Relief complete and satisfactory.Major W.H.L.Barnett,D.S.O. wounded.Situation normal,slightly increased activity of artillery.Patrols bring in correspondence as requested by Brigade.All coys. send Salvage down, leave party of 1 Officer & 11 O.R.s for England	APP I
	2nd		Battalion strengthens wire and improves trench.Enemy's T.M.s very active on "B" Coy. front 1 O.R.Killed 4 O.R.s Wounded	
	3rd		The G.O.C.& B.G.C. visit Battalion H.Q. Enemy shelling our posts with T.M.s 4 O.R.s Wounded	
	4th		Coys.improve trenches.Our artillery active on back areas 3 O.R.s Killed 6 O.Rs Wounded	
	5th		The Battalion shortens the frontage & are assisted mainly by the D.C.L.I.s,1 Coy R.Warwicks, with 1 Coy of R.W.Kents in support to the latter, no casualties	See 478,/570
	6th		The Battalion withdrew to ARCADE CAMP, refits baths & rests	
	7th		Church Parade at 11.0 a.m.	
	8th		The Battalion goes on an 8 mile route march & rests during the afternoon Major W.S.Chirnside M.C. arrives from England.	
	9th		During the morning training under Company arrangements,swimming sports in the afternoon. We win all the races - 50 yds,100yds & 250 yds.	
	10th		Training under Company arrangements.Boxing in the afternoon is interrupted by heavy rain	

Army Form C. 2118.

WAR DIARY
or
INTELLIGENCE SUMMARY

(Erase heading not required.)

Instructions regarding War Diaries and Intelligence Summaries are contained in F.S. Regs., Part II. and the Staff Manual respectively. Title Pages will be prepared in manuscript.

Place	Date	Hour	Summary of Events and Information	Remarks and references to Appendices
	July. 11th.		Wiring demonstration in the morning, and Concert. Battalion preparing for move to Support Line, Left Sector.	APP III
	12th.		Battalion moved up in support Lines in relief of the 2/K.O.S.B's. Relief went off well. One O.R. wounded. See P. 152	
	13th.		In support as above. Working party of One Officer and 30 O.R. found for R.E's. One Officer and 30 O.R. digging communication trench. 2/Lieut. E.C.Howlett, joined from 1st. Norfolks. Enemy Aircraft very active. 16 O.R. reinforcements from Reception Camp.	
	14th.		Still in Support. Found working parties for the R.E's. and digging communication trench to Front Line. Our heavies active in the afternoon, special attention being paid to MERVILLE.	
	15th.		Still in support. Our Artillery very active again to-day, but no reply from the enemy. Also found working parties.	
	16th.		Still in support. Artillery on our side still active, practically continuous day and night. Working parties found. Casualties - One O.R. wounded.	
	17th.		As above. Our artillery again very active. No retaliation from the enemy. General Birdwood and Staff visited Battalion Headquarters. Relieved 1st. Norfolks in front line in the ARREWAGE Sector. See P.O. 153	APP IV
	18th.		In front line as above. Morning early, one of our single seaters brought down by A.A. fire.	
	19th.		In front line. This morning 2 E.A. brought down, in aerial combat. One came down in flames, while the other crashed. Slight activity by the enemy artillery. (See App 154) APP XVI	
	20th.		At midnight "A" Coy. carried out a raid and attack. The raid was unsuccessful in that it did not yield any prisoners, but the attack was more successful. The enemy were driven back over the PLATE BECQUE which ran between us and the enemy. Casualties - 2/Lieut. H.W.Cornelius Killed, 2/Lieut. H.M.H.G.Blakeney wounded, 3 O.R. killed, 2 O.R. Missing, believed killed, and 10 O.R. wounded. Heavy enemy shelling during the raid, a heavy barrage of T.M's. were put up. One enemy balloon brought down by one of our 'Planes.	APP VI
	21st.		Still as above. Both artilleries fairly active.	
	22nd.		Still as above. The whole front remarkably quiet.	
	23rd.		Relieved by the 1st. Devons and withdrew to La Lacque Camp. See P.O. 155	APP VII
	24th.		In Camp as above. Whole Battalion cleaning up.	
	25th.		As above. Half the Battalion went bathing and the other half carried on with training under Coy. arrangements. In the evening, the whole Battalion went to a performance of the	

Army Form C. 2118.

WAR DIARY
or
INTELLIGENCE SUMMARY

(Erase heading not required.)

Place	Date	Hour	Summary of Events and Information	Remarks and references to Appendices
	26th.		"BEDFORD BOYS" in the Theatre of the Camp.	
	27th.		As above. Concert at night by the 1st. East Surrey Regtl. Troupe. (The Thirsty First)	
	28th.		As above. Concert at night by the 16th. R.Warwickshire troupe.	
			Church Parade in the Theatre. General Ponsonby, Divisional Commander, attended. The Divisional Band played.	
	29th.		Training carried on with. In the afternoon, Battalion Sports. Concert by the "BEDFORD BOYS" at night.	See OO 157 APP VIII
	30th.		Battalion preparing to move up in Brigade reserve at Villorba Camp. Move off 1 p.m.	
	31st.		Battalion started training in new Camp under Coy. arrangements. Also Coy's. had to build buttresses against huts to stop splinters from penetrating. "B" and "C" Coy's. found working parties.	

Lt. Colonel.

Commanding 1st. Battalion,
The Bedfordshire Regiment.

SECRET.   APP 1   Copy No.

OPERATION ORDER 150.

1st. Battalion The Bedfordshire Regiment.
Reference Map - France 36. A. N.E. 1/20,000.

July 4th. 1918.

1. The Battalion will be relieved by the 1st. Battalion D.C.L.I. on the night 5th./6th. July 1918. On relief, Companies will march by platoons to Acade Camp, (J.8.c.)
2. ROUTE. "B" and "C" Coy's. via the Halt, "D" and "A" Coy's. via Infantry Track from K.20.a.55.65. to K.13.b.25.75. All Companies then proceed along VIA ROMA and edge of Wood to l'Epinette and thence along main ST. VENANT Roadx - HAZEBROUCK Road to Arcade Camp. Guides will meet the Battalion on Main Road near Spresiano Camp.
3. GUIDES at the rate of one per platoon and one for Coy. H.Q. will be at Battalion H.Q. by 9.30 p.m. to-morrow night the 5th. inst to guide the 1st. D.C.L.I. to the line. These men must be certain of the exact route for their various platoons.
4. All Cooks utensils, Signallers kit, and Officers Mess Boxes, etc., will be dumped at the end of the light railway, K.13.b.7.9. by 9 p.m.
5. "B" and "C" Coy's. will meet their Lewis Gun Limber at The Halt. "D" and "A" Coy's. will meet their Lewis Gun Limber at the end of Infantry Track at K.13.b.35.75.
6. All trench stores, defence schemes, aeroplane photographs, and work in progress will be handed over and receipts obtained by Coy's.
7. Lists of stores to be handed over will reach Orderly Room with Intelligence Reports to-morrow morning.
8. Q.M. will arrange for a hot meal to be given to the troops on arrival at Arcade Camp
9. Q.M. will arrange to take over Arcade Camp to-morrow morning, and have guides to meet the Battalion outside Spresiano Camp at midnight.
10. Completion of relief will be reported by the words "LEATHER GUN" both by wire and runner. On arrival at Billets Coy's. will report present to Battalion Headquarters.

ACKNOWLEDGE.

R.H.O. Riddell   Lieut. & A/Adjt.
1st. Battalion Bedfordshire Regiment.

Copies to :-
1. H.Q., 15th. Infy. Bde.
2. O.C., 1st. D.C.L.I.
3. O.C. "A" Coy.
4.   " "B" "
5.   " "C" "
6.   " "D" "
7. T.O. & Q.M.
8. R.S.M.
9. File.
10.)
11.) War Diary.
12.)

APP III

SECRET.   OPERATION ORDER No. 158.   Copy No.

1st. Battalion The Bedfordshire Regt.

July 11th. 1916.

1. The 1st. Battalion Bedfordshire Regt. will relieve the 1/K.O.S.B's. in support in the left section of the Divisional front on the night of the 11th./12th. July 1916.

2. **DISPOSITIONS.** Companies will be distributed as follows :-
   "B" Coy. on the right, "C", "A" and "D" Coy. on the left.
   Companies will take over as follows :-
   "A" Bedfords from "A" Coy. K.O.S.B's.
   "B"   "   " "B" "   "
   "C"   "   " "C" "   "
   "D"   "   " "D" "   "

3. One Officer per Coy. and one N.C.O. per platoon will report to Orderly Room at 2 p.m. to proceed to the line to take over stores etc., and arrange distribution of platoons.

4. **GUIDES.** Guides at the rate of one per platoon and one for Coy. H.Q. will meet the Battalion at the end of No. 7 Infantry Track.

5. **ROUTE.** Via No. 7 Infantry track. Head of "B" Coy. to pass Headquarter board at 8.30 p.m. 100 yards between platoons and 250 yards between Companies. Order of march :-
   "B", "C", "A" and "D".

6. Officers valises, mens packs and surplus kit not wanted in the line will be dumped by Orderly Room by 6 p.m.
   Mess Boxes, Officers trench kits, Signalling kit and Cooks utensils for the line will be dumped by Orderly Room by 8 p.m.

7. **RATIONS.** Rations will be issued to the men before marching off, and will be carried to the line on the man.

8. Quartermaster will arrange to have 12 tins of water per Company sent up to-night and the tea same sent to Battalion Headquarters.

9. Lists of stores taken over must reach Orderly Room by 9 a.m. to-morrow the 12th. inst.

10. Completion of relief will be reported by wire by the name of C.S.M's.

ACKNOWLEDGE.

A.H.O. Riddell Lieut. & /Adjt.
1st. Battalion Bedfordshire Regiment.

Copies to :-
1. H.Q., 15th. Infy. Bde.   7. M.O.
2. O.C., 1/K.O.S.B.   8. T.O.
3. O.C. "A" Coy.   9. R.S.M.
4. " "B" "   10. File.
5. " "C" "   11.)
6. " "D" "   12.) War Diary.
                          13.

SECRET.   Copy No
         O P E R A T I O N   O R D E R   No. 153.
         ───
               1st. Battalion The Bedfordshire Regiment.
         ───
         Reference – Map, France, 36.A. N.E. Scale 1/20,000.
                                                    July 16th. 1918.
───

1. The Battalion will relieve the 1st. Battalion Norfolk Regt. in the
   right section of the ARREWAGE sector on the night of the 17th/18th.
   July 1918.
2. **Dispositions.** Coy's. will take over as follows :-
      "A" Coy. Left Front Line.   "C" Coy. Right Front Line.
      "D" Coy. Left Support.   "B" Coy. Right Support.
3. Company Commanders will arrange with their corresponding Company
   Commanders for guides. Companies to move off from their present
   positions as soon as it is dark. Battalion H.Q. will be at the Halt.
4. One Officer per Coy. will remain at present Coy. H.Q. to hand over to
   the 1st. Cheshire Regt. who are coming into our present position.
5. Guides at the rate of one per platoon and one for Coy. H.Q. will be
   sent to report to 1st. Cheshire H.Q. at Bristol Park (K.3.d.50.25)
   at 10 p.m. to guide the Cheshires to their positions.
6. List of stores taken over and rough sketch maps of new dispositions
   must reach Orderly Room with Intelligence reports on morning of 18th.
   July.
7. Rations will be brought up to Coy. H.Q. after relief.
8. Relief complete will be reported by the word "Potatoes" by wire.

        ACKNOWLEDGE.

                                R.H.O. Riddell   Lieut. & A/Adjt.
                          1st. Battalion Bedfordshire Regiment.

        Copies to :-
           1. H.Q., 15th. Infy. Bde.   8. Q.M. & T.O.
           2. O.C. 1st. Norfolks.   9. R.S.M.
           3. O.C. 1st. Cheshires.   10. File.
           4. O.C. "A" Coy.   11, 12 and 13. War Diary.
           5. "   "B" "
           6. "   "C" "
           7. "   "D" "

SECRET.   Copy No.
O P E R A T I O N   O N R D E R   No. 154.

            1st. Battalion Bedfordshire Regiment.

     Reference - Map, France 36.A. N.E. Scale 1/20,000.
                                                            July 19th. 1918.

1. The enemy will be cleared from all the ground formed by triangle between
    our front line, the PLATE BECQUE, and R.BOURRE. As many prisoners as
    possible will be captured and brought back alive.
2. "A" Coy. will carry out this operation to-night 19th/20th. with the
    support of Artillery, 6" Newtons, Stokes Mortars and Machine Guns.
3. The raid will be carried out by two platoons in two waves. First wave
    consisting of 4 rifle sections, and second wave two Lewis Gun sections.
    One Officer will be put in command of each wave. Boundary between the
    two waxes platoons will be the road running up to the footbridge
    inclusive to right platoon.
    One platoon will follow up in support but will not be used unless
    opposition is encountered. One platoon will remain in reserve in our
    front line.
4. The two assaulting platoons will assemble with first wave 40 yards
    outside our wire, and second wave 20 yards behind the first. The
    supporting platoon will keep in the front line until zero hour.
    Assembly will be complete by 11.40 p.m.
5. The objective will be a line 50 yards East and parallel to the German
    trench running from KxKxxxxxxx. K.16.c.50.50. to K.16.a.80.60. but
    any enemy still remaining this side of the PLATE BECQUE will be rounded
    up.
6. Dress will be fighting order. Each rifleman will carry two Mills.
    Wire cutters will be carried by every man in the front wave.
7. ARTILLERY PROGRAMME. Artillery barrage will be put down at Zero hour on
    enemy positions between K.16.b.25.30. round the junction of PLATE BECQUE
    and R.BOURRE to bend of R.BOURRE at K.16.c.30.20. and along enemy position
    from this Point to Gurnard Cross K.21.b.50.60. One Thermite round in
    every five will be fired on the following points to give direction of
    the two flanks and centre of the raid. Right on line of R.BOURRE
    running through K.22.b.xxxxxxx centre on Les Pures Becque left at K.16.d.
    60.90. Rate of fire for the first 20 minutes will be intense, will
    slacken down for the next ten minutes, and finally die down after a
    further ten minutes. Total - 40 minutes fire.
8. Stokes Mortars will shoot on enemy positions from K.21.b.50.60. to
    K.21.b.99.99.
9. 6" Newtons will fire on the line between RENNET FARM and PURES BECQUE.
10. Machine Guns will enfilade the enemy position between K.16.b.25.30. and
    K.16.d.30.80.
11. Watches will be synchronised at 8 p.m.
12. Zero hour will be 12 midnight, but the raid will not start before the
    Artillery barrage is put down.
13. All clear will be signalled by 3 GREEN Very lights.

14. **General.** The raid will be carried out with the utmost rapidity and vigour. It will be impressed on all ranks that as many prisoners as possible are to brought in and that no uncaptured enemy are to remain on our side of PLATE BECQUE.
The places where the enemy will probably be found are in post at K.16.c.50.50. probable post at road K.16.c.70.80. and probable working party about K.16.central. No papers or letters will be carried nor numerals worn.

ACKNOWLEDGE.

N.W.O.Riddell Lieut. & A/Adjt.
1st. Battalion Bedfordshire Regiment.

Copies to :-
1. H.Q. 15th. Infy. Bde.
2. O.C. "A" Coy.
3. " "B" "
4. " "C" "
5. " "D" "
6. O.C. "C" Coy. M.G. Bn.
7. O.C., T.M.Bty.
8. O.C. 6" Newtons.
9. O.C. Left Coy. R.F.A.
10. File.
11., 12 and 13. War Diary.

SECRET.

Copy No. APP VII

OPERATION ORDER No. 156.

1st. Battalion Bedfordshire Regiment.

July 23rd. 1918.

1. The 1st. Bn. Bedfordshire Regt. will be relieved by the 1st. Bn. The Devonshire Regt. on the night of 23rd./24th. July 1918. On relief, the Battalion will move into La Lacque Camp.
2. Each platoon on being relieved will proceed to the Halt, where they will entrain on the light railway. The police under Lt. Nailer will superintend the entrainment.
3. Q.M. will arrange guides to meet trains at La Lacque station at the rate of one per platoon to guide them to their huts.
4. Coy's. will arrange to send guides at the rate of one per platoon and one per Coy. H.Q. to report at Battalion Headquarters by 9 p.m. to guide the incoming Unit into the line. These guides must be certain of the route to their various platoons.
5. Lewis Guns will be taken on the train.
6. Battalion Cooks utensils will be ready to go down on R.E. train by 3 p.m. Q.M. will arrange to meet these at HARTSTONE Station.
7. Two Limbers, Officers Mess Cart, and Medical Cart will be at the Halt by 9.30 p.m.
8. The following Transport will move to La Lacque Camp :-
   All Chargers, Officers Mess and Medical Carts and Lewis Gun Limbers.
9. Lists of trench stores to be handed over must reach Orderly Room by 12 noon.
10. A hot meal will be issued to the troops on arrival at La Lacque.
11. Completion of relief will be reported by the code words "Send Rum" by wire. Company Commanders will call at the Halt as they pass.

ACKNOWLEDGE.

A.N.O. Riddell. Lieut. & A/Adjt.
1st. Battalion Bedfordshire Regiment.

Copies to :-
1. H.Q. 15th. Infy. Bde.
2. O.C. 1st. Devons.
3. O.C. "A" Coy.
4. " "B" "
5. " "C" "
6. " "D" "
7. Q.M. & T.O.
8. R.S.M.
9. File.
10.)
11.) War Diary.
12.)

SECRET.

Copy No.....

OPERATION ORDER No. 157.

1st. Battalion The Bedfordshire Regiment.
Map Reference - Sheet 36.A. N.E. Scale 1/20,000 Ed. 7.

July 29th. 1918.

1. The Battalion will relieve the 15th. Battalion The R.Warwickshire Regt. in reserve in the LE SART Section on the afternoon of the 30th. July 1918.
2. The Battalion will march in the following order :-
    H.Q., "D", "B", "C" and "A".
    100 yards between platoons and 200 yards between Companies.
    H.Q. to pass Officers Mess at 1 p.m.
    Special attention will be paid to March Discipline.
3. ROUTE. Road South of Camp, through squares I.32.b., I.27.c., I.33.b., across railway and ferry to main Tannay Road. Thence to road at I.26.b.4.5. - alongedge of wood to l'Epinette and Villorba Camp.
4. 2/Lieut. H.J.Snashall and 4 C.Q.M.Sgts and Sgt. Thurley will proceed to Villorba Camp to-morrow morning to take over from the 15th. R.Warwicks.
    2/Lieut. W.Haynes and One N.C.O. per Coy. will stay to hand over La Lacque Camp to the incoming Unit.
5. C.Q.M.Sgts will meet their Companies at the entrance to Villorba Camp, to guide them into their Huts.
6. Lewis Guns will be taken on Limbers. Sgt. Faulder will be responsible for the loading.
7. Officers Valises, Officers and Sergeants Mess Boxes, Orderly Room and Canteen Boxes will be collected at 1.30 p.m. Transport Officer will arrange to have these picked up and taken to Villorba Camp One servant per Coy. and one for Coy. H.. will remain with these kits.
8. Rations will be issued at Villorba Camp.
9. Companies will report at Battalion Headquarters at Villorba Camp when their Coy's. are all in.

ACKNOWLEDGE.

A.r.o Ridsall Capt. & Adjt.
1st. Battalion The Bedfordshire Regiment.

Copies to :-
    H.Q., 15th. Infy. Bde.   Q.M.
    O.C. 15th. R.Warwickshire Regt. T.O.
    O.C. "A" Coy.   R.S.M.
     "   "B" "   File.
     "   "C" "   War Diary.
     "   "D" "

1st Bedfordshire Regt

August 1918

Volume No. _____

BRITISH SALONIKA FORCE

WAR DIARY.

Vol. No.	Unit	PERIOD From	To
30.	No. 3 Base M.T. Depot, A.S.C.	1.4.18	30.4.18
19.	No. 4 Advanced M.T. Depot, A.S.C.	1.4.18	30.4.18
16.	208 M.T. Coy. A.S.C.	"	"
16.	209. do.	"	"
19.	238 do.	"	"
19.	29th Reserve Park, A.S.C.	"	"
20.	369 M.T. Coy. A.S.C.	"	"
14.	798 do.	"	"
16.	799 M.T. Coy. A.S.C.	"	"
13.	800 do.	"	"
4.	"A" Provisional M.T. Coy. A.S.C.	1.4.18	10.4.18

CONFIDENTIAL.

Register............. 5
Part No............. 5/15
Volume No........... [illegible] 46

WAR DIARY

OF

1st Bn. Bedfordshire Regt.

for the month of

August -------- 1918.

[signature] Cooper
Lt. & A/Capt. 1st Bn. Beds Regt.
Commanding

3/9/1918.

Army Form C. 2118.

WAR DIARY
or
INTELLIGENCE SUMMARY

(Erase heading not required.)

Instructions regarding War Diaries and Intelligence Summaries are contained in F. S. Regs., Part II. and the Staff Manual respectively. Title Pages will be prepared in manuscript.

Place	Date	Hour	Summary of Events and Information	Remarks and references to Appendices
	AUGUST 1918			
	1st.		Battalion in VILLORBA Camp, in the early morning Camp was shelled with gas and H.E. and shrapnel. Casualties, 5 Other Ranks gassed. Working parties found on Divisional Line, BEDFORD & CHESHIRE Communication Trenches, also roads and tracks in vicinity of Camp.	
	2nd		Enemy artillery fairly active at night and early morning. H.V.guns shelled TANNAY and some fell around ARCADE Camp. Not so much gas shell used. The usual working parties found.	
	~~XXX~~ 3rd		Raining hard all day.	
			In Camp as above, usual working parties found and usual early morning artillery activity around Camp.	
	4th		As above, 3 Companies on working party, 1 Company on Church Parade (Remembrance Day) Lieut. J.P.KINGDON to 5th Army School as instructor. Capt.& Adjt., A.H.O.RIDDELL & Lieut.E.I.F.NALLER to leave in country. Usual enemy shelling in vicinity of Camp.	
	5th		As above, working parties found as usual. Warning Order for relief received & Operation Order for move on following day.	
	6th		Preparing for move to LA LACQUE Camp at night, Battalion left VILLORBA at 6.35 p.m. and arrived at LA LACQUE at 8.30.p.m. See O.O.158	App.1.
	7th		Enemy aircraft bombing in vicinity of Camp during night. Marched to BLARINGHEM and billetted (Area C). Billets in very poor condition. Battalion employed bathing. Au O.O. 159	APP II
	8th		Billetted as above, Battalion Training commenced. Football in the afternoon.	
	9th		In billets as above, Brigadier General R.D.F.Oldman inspected the Battalion. Games in afternoon.	
	10th		In billets as above, training continued.	
	11th		As above, Church Services for all denominations.	
	12th		Received Warning Order to move at any moment.	
	13th		As above, "D"Company moved to WIZERNES Station to act as loading party. Remainder of Battalion preparing for move.	
	14th		Battalion marched to WIZERNES Station and entrained. Detrained at DOULLENS and marched to OUTREBOIS and billetted. Au O.O 160	APP III
	15th		In billets as above, Battalion employed bathing.	
	16th		In billets as above, Battalion moved in the afternoon to REMAISNIL and billetted. Au O.O.161	APP IV

WAR DIARY or INTELLIGENCE SUMMARY

Army Form C. 2118.

Place	Date	Hour	Summary of Events and Information	Remarks and references to Appendices
	17th		Billetted as above, training carried on.	
	18th		In billets as above, received warning order to move at short notice. Battalion marched to ORVILLE and billetted for one night. Dumped Personnel (8 Officers and 87 Other Ranks) were sent back to DOULLENS.	
	19th		Battalion marched to SAILLY au BOIS and billetted for the night in ruined houses. Raining during whole of the march.	
	20th		As above, Brigade Operation Order received for move to forward position ready to take part in the attack. Battalion moved up at 8.55 p.m. to assembly position near BUCQUOY.	App VI Act 00162
	21st		Battalion moved forward to the attack at 4.45 a.m. meeting with very slight opposition. The objective was about 1500 yards from original German Front Line, which had already been taken by the 37th Division. Battalion gained objective which they consolidated, remaining in support to 1st Norfolk Regiment, who passed through to take the next objective. Casualties - Captains G. de C.MILLAIS & H.J.WEST M.C. wounded (since Died) and 46 Other Ranks Killed & Wounded etc.	
	22nd		Battalion still in support. Enemy shelling heavily with gas shells. Casualties - Lieut.W.M.STANTAN (Attd.T.M.B.) Wounded and 2/Lieut.H.MAW Killed.	
	23rd		Battalion moved up in front of ACHIET le PETIT and moved forward to the attack at 11 a.m. All objectives taken, Battalion suffered rather heavily from Machine Gun fire. Casualties - Officers Killed Lieut.G.ABBOTT " H.J.A.WATSON " E.I.F.NAILER " A.R.C.EATON " R.H.ARNHOLZ 2/Lieut.F.H.FOX " W.T.PAINE Officers Wounded Lt.Col.;H.COURTENAY M.C. (since died) 2/Lieut.H.J.SNASHALL " F.J.KELF 129 Other Ranks Killed and Wounded etc.	

WAR DIARY
or
INTELLIGENCE SUMMARY

(Erase heading not required.)

Army Form C. 2118

Instructions regarding War Diaries and Intelligence Summaries are contained in F. S. Regs., Part II. and the Staff Manual respectively. Title Pages will be prepared in manuscript.

Place	Date	Hour	Summary of Events and Information	Remarks references to Appendices
	24th 25th		Battalion withdrew to Brown Line in reserve. Battalion in reserve in Brown Line. As above. At 9 a.m. Battalion moved forward to trenches two kilimetres in front of ACHIET le PETTIT still in reserve.	
	26th 27th		Battalion still in reserve.	
	28th		As above. Battalion and "A" & "B" Echelons of Transport moved forward. Transport in front of ACHIET le PETTIT, Battalion in vicinity of BAPAUME. Draft of 62 Other Ranks joined Battalion from Base Depot.	
	29th 30th		As above, Battalion standing to ready to move at a moment's notice. Battalion situated as above.	
	31st		As above, Usual artillery activity.	

1/9/18

[signature] Lieut. for O.C.
1st Battalion The Bedfordshire Regiment.

SECRET.   APP I   Copy No. 14

OPERATION ORDER No. 156.

1st. Battalion Bedfordshire Regiment.

August 5th. 1918.

1. The Battalion will withdraw to La Lacque Camp on the evening of the 6th/7th. August 1918.
2. Order of March:- Headquarters, "D", "C", "B" and "A" Coy. 100 yards between Companies. Head of column will leave the Camp at 6.30 p.m.
3. ROUTE - Along edge of wood to Road at J.20.d.2.2. to main TANNAY Road, - Road at I.29.a.0.5., cross Ferry and Railway to La Lacque Camp. Drums will meet the Battalion at a point where the Battalion strike the main Tannay Road.
4. C.Q.M.Sgts. will report to 2/Lieut. L.J.Hobson at Transport Lines at 8 a.m. on the morning of the 6th. where they will proceed to La Lacque to take over from the 1st. Devonshire Regt. arriving at 9 a.m.
5. Details at Transport Lines will march independently under 2/Lieut. W. Haynes to La Lacque Camp, arriving there at 7 p.m.
   2/Lieut. W.Haynes will provide guides from these details to meet the Battalion at the entrance to La Lacque Camp, and guide them to their Huts. One guide per platoon.
6. Guards at Forest Corner, J.21.central and l'Epinette, (J.21.a.6.6.) will be withdrawn by the R.S.M. at 4 p.m. if they are not relieved before.
7. Lewis Guns will be taken from Villorba Camp on L.G.Limbers. Sgt. Foulder will superintend the loading of these.
8. Personnel of Brigade Pioneer Coy. will rejoin Unit at La Lacque Camp.
9. Officers Valises, Mess Boxes, Orderly Room Boxes and Canteen Boxes will be ready for loading at 4.30 p.m. sharp. Transport Officer will arrange for necessary Transport for these to be at the Camp by 5 p.m.
10. Rations will be sent to La Lacque Camp, and will be distributed before breakfast on the morning of the 7th. inst.
11. O.C. Coy's. and R.S.M., will report present or otherwise to Battalion Headquarters at La Lacque Camp, immediately on arrival.

ACKNOWLEDGE.

                                                    James Meade
                                                    2/Lieut. & A/Adjt.
                                                    1st. Battalion Bedfordshire Regiment.

Copies to :-
1. H.Q., 15th. Infy. Bde.   6. T.O.
2. OFC. "A" Coy.   7. Q.M.
3. "   "B" "   8. 2/Lt. W.Haynes and 2/Lt. L.J.Hobson.
4. "   "C" "   9. R.S.M.
5. "   "D" "   10. Sgt. Dmr. F.J.Coe.
                                 11. File.
                                 12, 13, and 14. War Diary.

Aug 1918

Aug. 1918

App. II.

OPERATION ORDER No 159.

Copy No.

1st. Battalion Bedfordshire Regiment.

Aug. 7th. 1918.

1. The Battalion will march to ~~the Training~~ Area "C" North of BLARINGHAM.
2. Head of column will pass starting point, (Officers Mess) at 2 p.m.
   Order of march :-
   Drums, H.Q., "A", "B", "C" and "D".
   100 yards between Companies, and between Rear Coy. and Transport.
3. ROUTE. Drawbridge at I.32.a.4.5. - AIRE Station - WITTES - BLARINGHAM. - RENESCURE Road. Strict march discipline will be maintained.
4. The Transport moving direct from TANNAY will join the rear of the column at Drawbridge at I.32.a.4.5.
5. Dinners will be at ~~12 noon.~~ 11-45 am. Teas on arrival.
6. All Companies will be clear of the huts at 1 p.m. to enable the Medical Officer to make an inspection.
7. Officers Valises and Mess Boxes will be loaded by 1.30 pm.
8. O.C. Coy's. and R.S.M. will report Battalion present or otherwise immediately on arrival in the new area.

ACKNOWLEDGE.

James Meade
2/Lieut. & A/Adjt.
1st. Battalion Bedfordshire Regiment.

Copies to :-
O.C. "A" Coy.
" "B" "
" "C" "
" "D" "
T.O.
Q.M.
R.S.M.

File
War Diary.

SECRET.   App III
                                                                        Copy No.
                    O P E R A T I O N   O R D E R   No. 160.
                    ───
                        1st. Battalion The Bedfordshire Regiment.
        Ref. Map - HAZEBROUCK 5A. Edition 2, Scale 1/100,000.
                                                              August 13th. 1918.
──

1. The Battalion will move to-morrow the 14th. inst to the Third Army Area
    by train, marching to WIZERNES Station.
2. ROUTE - WARDRECQUES - BLARART - LE ROQUET - BLENDECQUES - WIZERNES.
3. REVEILLE. Reveille will be at 6 a.m. Sick parade at 6.30 a.m.
        Breakfasts at 7 a.m.
4. STARTING POINT. Head of column will pass starting point, (Road Junction
    immediately South of the first P in N.WD- POSES) at 8.30 a.m.
        Order of march - Headquarters, Drums, C, B and A Coy's.
    Transport will move off at 8.15 a.m. and will not accompany
    the Battalion. They will be in advance.
    The Drums will change to the next Company in rear at each Halt.
5. Officers Kits, Mess Boxes, Orderly Room Boxes, Canteen Boxes, etc., will
    be ready for loading at 7 a.m. Officers Kits etc., will be stacked
    outside Coy. Headquarters, and Transport will call for them on the march.
6. DINNERS will be served at WIZERNES Station on arrival, before entrainment,
    about 11.45 a.m.
7. TENTAGE. All Tents, Bivouac Sheets, etc., will be struck immediately
    after reveille. These will be collected by the Transport Officer, and
    handed over to the Area Commandant. Receipts will be obtained.
8. BILLETING PARTY. The Billeting party detailed in this office A.760,
    dated 13/8/18, will rendezvous at "B" Coy's. Headquarters at 7 a.m.
    They will proceed to ARQUES Station, arriving there at 8 a.m. They
    will proceed by train No. 16, leaving at 9.27 a.m.
9. Orderly Officer for to-morrow - 2/Lieut. W.Haynes.

                                                James Meade
ACKNOWLEDGE.   2/Lieut. & A/Adjt.
                        1st. Battalion Bedfordshire Regiment.

Copies to :-
    1. H.Q. 15th. Infty. Bde.
    2. O.C. "A" Coy.
    3. "   "B" "
    4. "   "C" "
    5. "   "D" "
    6. T.O.
    7. Q.M.
    8. R.S.M.
    9. 2/Lieut. A.B.F.Sheldrake.
    10. File.
    11.)
    12.) War Diary.
    13.)

SECRET.   Copy No.
                    O P E R A T I O N   O R D E R   No. 161.

                    1st. Battalion The Bedfordshire Regiment.
         Ref. Map. - LENS 11. Scale 1/100,000.
                                                        August 16th. 1918.

1. The Battalion will move into billets at REMAISNIL this afternoon the
    16th. inst.
2. ROUTE - To Cross Roads immediately south of the SX xx Kxxxx 11 in
    Mezerolles, turn to the left to the village of Mezerolles, thence to the
    Right to Remaisnil.
3. The Battalion will form up in the following order :-
         H.Q., Drums, "D", "C", "A" and "B", Stretcher Bearers, Transport.
    Head of column to be on bridge across river by Battalion Orderly Room,
    facing North, ready to move off by 4 p.m.
4. ADVANCE PARTY. One Sgt. per Coy, and one for H.Q., and one for Q.M's
    stores and Transport, will report to Orderly Room at 10 a.m. to proceed
    to take over billets at Remaisnil.
5. Officers Kits, Mess Boxes, Orderly Room Boxes, Canteen Boxes, etc., will
    be stacked outside billets ready to pick up by 2 p.m.
6. Certificates to the effect that billets are left clean will be handed to
    the Adjutant before moving off by Companies.

    ACKNOWLEDGE.
                                                                Capt. & Adjt.
                    1st. Battalion Bedfordshire Regiment.

Copies to :-
    1. H.Q., 15th. Infy.Bde.   6. T.O.   10. Lieut. G.Abbott.
    2. O.C. "A" Coy.   7. Q.M.   11, 12, and 13.
    3.   "   "B" "   8. R.S.M.   War Diary.
    4.   "   "C" "   9. File.
    5.   "   "D" "

SECRET.

OPERATION ORDER No. 162.

1st. Battalion The Bedfordshire Regiment.
Ref. Maps. Scale 1/20,000.   57.D. N.E. and 57.C. N.
August 20th. 1918.

---

1. The Third Army has been ordered to press the enemy back towards BAPAUME, and to prevent him from destroying the railways and communications.
The initial attack on the 4th. Corps front will be made by the 37th. Div. whose objective will be the BLUE Line.   The 5th. Div. with the 63rd. Div. on its left will pass through and capture the BROWN and RED Lines.   The 5th. Division will attack with the 95th. Bde. on the right and the 15th. Bde. on the left., the 13th. Bde. being in reserve.
The 13th. Bde. will attack with the 1st. Bedfords on the right and the 1st. Norfolks on the left. 16th. Warwicks in rear of 1st. Bedfords, and the 1st. Cheshires in rear of 1st. Norfolks.   The boundaries and of objectives allotted to the Battalion are shown on the maps already issued to Companies.

2. ASSEMBLY POSITION. The Battalion will assemble on a line, KEANE and CROSS trenches, the right boundary being H in KEANE TRENCH, left boundary, ESSARTS-BUCQUOY Road, in touch with 1st. Norfolks on far side of the road.

3. PLAN OF ATTACK.   The Battalion will attack with "C" and "D" Coy's in the front line, each Coy. with two platoons in the front wave, and two in support.   "D" Coy. will be on the right, and "C" Coy. on the left. "B" Coy. will be in support, holding two platoons to support each of the front line Coy's.   "A" Coy. will be reserve.
At zero hour, the Battalion will leave its assembly position, and advance to the Eastern side of BUCQUOY to about a line L.9.b.3.8. to L.3.d.9.5. The formation during this move will be in Artillery Formation, with platoons in file.   Here they will re-assemble with the two leading Coy's. in Artillery formation of blobs of sections in file.   Support and reserve Coy's. will remain in original formation, unless enemy shelling is heavy, when they will break up in section blobs, at the discretion of Company Commanders.   During the move between these two assembly positions the left leading platoon of "D" Coy. will guide.
Great care must be taken to keep in touch with this platoon, as the ground through the village is broken and enclosed.   At zero plus 65 minutes, the Battalion will advance, and cross the BLUE objective at zero plus 90 minutes.   This advance will be covered by Tanks.
The leading Coy's. will keep as close to the Tanks as possible.   Rate of advance - 100 yards in 4 minutes.
The distance between the leading Coy's. and the support Coy's. will be 100 yards.
At zero plus 162 minutes, the 16th. R.Warwicks will pass through the Battalion, and advance to their final dotted RED Line objective.
When touch has been obtained with troops on both flanks, and the 16th. Warwicks and 1st. Cheshires have passed over the BROWN Line, the Battalion will side slip and take over the whole of the BROWN Line with "C" and "D" Coy's., the 1st. Norfolks being withdrawn.
"A" and "B" Coy's. will form up in the trench line running through L.11.b and d.   "B" Coy. on the left.   "A" Coy. on the right.
Consolidation will then be immediately started on the BROWN Line.
MACHINE GUNS.   One section of "C" Coy. 5th. M.G.Battn. is allotted to the Battalion and will advance with the support Coy. On arrival at the BROWN objective, O.C. of the section will select positions to cover this line while it is being consolidated.   He must also be prepared to support the attacking Companies during the advance if the necessity arises.
STOKES GUNS.   8 Stokes Guns will also be attached to the Battalion, and will move forward during the attack with the support Coy.
ARTILLERY.   The advance from the BLUE to the BROWN objective will be covered by a creeping barrage of Field Artillery, which will cease at

Zero plus 162 minutes.

TANKS. For the capture of the BROWN Line, 6 Mark IV Tanks are allotted to the Brigade. One of these will move up between the two parallel trench lines running along our right boundary.

TANK SIGNALS. Tanks to Infantry.
    WHITE and GREEN FLAG – Come to me.
    RED and YELLOW FLAG – Am out of action. Go on without me.
    RED, WHITE and BLUE FLAG – Am withdrawing. Don't shoot.

Infantry to Tanks.
    Helmet waved on rifle – Come to me.

4. ORDER OF MARCH. Headquarters, "C", "D", "B" and "A" Coy's. Headquarters will move off at 8.55 p.m. Interval between Coy's. 100 yards.

5. GUIDES. Guides of the New Zealand Divn. at the rate of 2 per Coy. and 5 for Battalion Headquarters will be picked up at SAILLY-au-BOIS Church. These guides will take Coy's. as far as the South corner of ROSSIGNOL Farm and on from there to the assembly area, guides of the 37th. Divn. will lead Coy's.

6. LEWIS GUN LIMBERS. The L.G.Limbers will march in the rear of each Coy. Lewis Guns will be taken off the Limbers on arriving just East of GOMMECOURT.

7. CONTACT PLANES. A Contact Plane will fly over the attacking Infantry and call for flares.
At zero plus 3 hours, "C" and "D" Coy's. light flares.
   "   " 5 "   Battalion will not light flares.
   "   " 7 "   Anyone lights flares.
The Signal from the plane to denote assembly of hostile counter attack will be the dropping of a RED Smoke Bomb.

8. LIAISON. Close touch must be kept with the troops on either flank.

9. BATTALION HEADQUARTERS. Battn. H.Q. during the assembly will be at the junction of ROSSIGNOL Avenue, and BROWN Trench.
When the Battalion moves forward to second assembly position, East of BUCQUOY, Battn. H.Q. will be established in the trench about L.4.c.1.1.
When the attacking troops reach the BROWN objective, Battn. H.Q. will be established in the trench about L.11.d.6.7.

10. MOPPING UP. "A" Coy. will systematically mop up the system of trenches running parallel to the line of our advance up to the BROWN Line.
"B" Coy. will keep a sharp lookout for any pockets that may be missed during the advance of the leading Coy's. and mop these up.

11. SYNCHRONISATION. Watches will be synchronised at Battalion Headquarters at 7.30 p.m. Zero hour will be notified later.

12. SIGNALS. (a) One Very light will be fired by order of Coy. Commander on the capture of BROWN objective, and two in succession on the capture of the RED.
(b) The S.O.S. Signal will be RED over GREEN over RED.

13. DUMPS. Tools for the consolidation of the BROWN Line will be dumped at a point on the BUCQUOY–ACHIET-le-PETIT Road where the BROWN line crosses it. In addition to this, arrangements have been made for the Tanks to bring up as many shovels as possible, and to dump these on the BROWN Line, but it is not expected that more than 50 shovels will be brought up by Tanks.

14. DRESS. Dress will be Fighting order.

15. RATIONS. Rations for the 21st. and the 22nd. will be carried, in addition to the Iron Ration. Each man will also carry one tin of solidified alcohol.

16. BANDOLIERS AND TRENCH STORES. Each man will carry 2 sandbags and one extra bandolier of S.A.A. 20 magazines per Lewis Gun will be carried. Grenades, Wire Cutters, Very Lights, Flares and S.O.S. Signals will be distributed to Companies as available.

17. RUM. Rum will be issued at zero minus one hour.

18. DRESSING STATION. will be established at Battn. H.Q. in each position.

                                                Capt. & Adjt.
                                      1st. Battalion Bedfordshire Regiment.

15/5

1st Bedfordshire Regt

September 1918.

Volume No. ____

BRITISH SALONIKA FORCE

WAR DIARY.

Vol. No.	Unit	PERIOD From	To
8.	95th Labour Company.	1. 6. 18.	30. 6. 18
8.	96th Labour Company	1. 6. 18.	30. 6. 18
11.	98th Labour Company	1. 6. 18.	30. 6. 18
7.	201st Labour Company.	1. 6. 18.	30. 6. 18

To
Headquarters
15th Infantry Brigade.

Herewith War Diary for March 1919.

W. E. Searle, Major.
Commanding 1st Battalion The Bedfordshire Regiment.

WAR DIARY

OF

1st Bedfordshire Regt

for the month of
September 1918.

WAR DIARY
or
INTELLIGENCE SUMMARY
(Erase heading not required.)

Army Form C. 2118.

Place	Date	Hour	Summary of Events and Information	Remarks and references to Appendices
	1/8		Battalion moved up to Railway line in vicinity of FREMICOURT and dug in	
	2/8	5.15am	Battalion advanced to the attack (in reserve) in front of FREMICOURT - Lieut. G.G. Mayes wounded. 94 Other ranks killed, wounded and missing.	App. I.
	3/8		"B" & "D" bombers sent forward to the attack and found that the enemy had evacuated the position. These two companies advanced about four miles until they came in contact with the enemy, they then dug in. Relieved at night and marched back to LE SUCQUIERE and encamped. Casualties: 9 other ranks wounded.	
	4/8		Battalion withdrew to camp near BIEFVILLERS	App. II
	5/8		In camp as above employed in clearing up and refitting.	
	6/8		In camp as above. Battalion training commenced.	
	7/8 8/8 9/8 10/8 11/8		Do above - Training carried on. Weather wet very so no no wards	

Army Form C. 2118.

WAR DIARY
or
INTELLIGENCE SUMMARY
(Erase heading not required.)

Instructions regarding War Diaries and Intelligence Summaries are contained in F. S. Regs., Part II. and the Staff Manual respectively. Title Pages will be prepared in manuscript.

Place	Date	Hour	Summary of Events and Information	Remarks and references to Appendices
	12/8		As above. The following officers joined the Battalion. Lieut. D. 15. Y. Branwick. Lieut. L. D. Y. Harvey. 2Lieut. L. A. Clarke. — J Blakely Knight. — E. D. Q. Robinson. — B. D. Shinn. — J. A. Trotor. — J. D. Blackwell. — L. J. Cole	
	13/8		As above. Training carried on.	
	14/8		In camp as above. Received "Warning Orders to move up into Divisional Reserve.	
	15/8		Moved up into VILLA au FLOS in the morning and billeted in Huts and tng-pit. Enemy air-craft very active bombing vicinity of village at night.	App. III
	16/8		In Billets as above. Training carried on under Brigade arrangements. Enemy active with H.V. Guns.	
	17/8			
	18/8			
	19/8		In Divisional Reserve as above. Warned to be ready to move at half an hours notice.	
	20/8		Received Warning Order to move. Moved at night to BARASTRE and BUS. Battalion relieved at VILLIERS au FLOS by 2nd Bn. K.O.S.B. and relieved 1st Bn. D.C.L.I at YTRES. Some shelling by H.V. Guns in vicinity of railway at YTRES.	App. IV

WAR DIARY
or
INTELLIGENCE SUMMARY

Army Form C. 2118.

Place	Date	Hour	Summary of Events and Information	Remarks and references to Appendices
	21/9/18		In bomb so above. Enemy H.V. Guns very active throughout.	
	22/9/18		In bomb so above. Shew of enemy fire of ammunition. H.V. Guns again active. Hostile T.M. shoots around a number and died later in the day.	
	23/9/18		As above. Enemy enemy shelling around Camp.	
	24/9/18		As above.	
	25/9/18		As above. Brigade O.O. issued to nest for following day. Battalion preparation in readiness.	
	26/9/18		Battalion received orders to move into assembly position ready for forthcoming operations.	
	27/9/18	4.52am	Battalion advanced on H hour to attack and capture part of BEAUCAMP VILLAGE. All objectives taken. Enemy heavy barrage brought down during advance. Entry to attack followed. Messages to Linden Trench temporarily known as VILLAGE. Casualties:— Capt. R.E. Schaal, Lieut. Elge, R.H.H. Catell, R.H. Patchett, 2/Lt. H.T. Thomas, 2/Lt. Lushington killed 9 Wounded, 2/Lt. G.N. Blackwell, 19 missing. Other Ranks 19 killed, 95 Wounded, 11 missing.	R/p I.
	28/9/18		Remained in captured BEAUCAMP. Enemy shoots around trenches.	
			2/Lt.G.G. Mitchell Wounded returned to duty. Other Ranks — 1 killed + 5 wounded.	

WAR DIARY
or
INTELLIGENCE SUMMARY

Army Form C. 2118.

Place	Date	Hour	Summary of Events and Information	Remarks and references to Appendices
	29/8		Battn. passed through 95th Brigade, attacked by a Railway and consolidated. 2/2 K.R.T. Ramdruck Wounded. 2nd Lt. Hulley slight. Lt. on duty. Other Ranks – 1 killed, 2 died of wds., 8 wounded, 2 missing.	
	30/8		Remains during Battalion moved forward. Relieved in evening by 13th K.R.R., 34th Division and withdrew to DEAD MAN'S CORNER. Casualties – 5 wounded, 1 & 2 died of wounds.	

SECRET.   Copy No. 10.
              O P E R A T I O N   O R D E R   No. 168.

                    1st. Battalion The Bedfordshire Regiment.
                                                    Sept. 1st. 1918.

1. On Sept. 2nd. the advance will be continued resumed by the 15th. Infantry Brigade in conjunction with Divisions on either flank.
2. The attack of the 15th. Infantry Brigade will be carried out on a two Battalion front as follows :-
       1st. Norfolks   -   Right.
       1st. Cheshires   -   Left.
       16th. R.Warwicks -   In support, (Left)
       1st. Bedfords   -   In reserve, (Right)
   The attack will be preceded by an Artillery barrage which will open on the line I.21.c.3.0. to I.9.c.3.0. where it will remain for four minutes before creeping forward.
3. The objectives allotted to the 15th. Infantry Brigade are as follows :-
       1st. Objective.
              I.28.a.1.1. round Eastern edge of BEUGNY - I.16.a.8.5.
       2nd. Objective.
              I.34.b.8.8. - I.29. central. - I.17.d.5.7. - (Factory)
   The dividing line between Battalions will be the normal guage railway through I.21. - I.22.c. - I.28.b. - and I.29.a.
   The 1st. Norfolks and 1st. Cheshires will be responsible for the capture of both objectives.
4. The general rate of advance to the 1st. objective will be 100 yards in 4 minutes.
   A halt of one hour will be made on the line of the 1st. objective.
   The signal for the advance to the 2nd. objective to commence will be the opening of the Artillery barrage, which will only take place if the 62nd. Division (on left) have captured MORCHIES.
   If the 62nd. Division fail to capture MORCHIES, the barrage for the advance to the 2nd. objective will not open, and no further advance will be made.
5. (a) MACHINE GUNS. 1 section of "C" Coy. M.G.Battn. will advance with Battalion.
   (b) TANKS. 2 Tanks, (Mark IV) will assist in mopping up BEUGNY and will advance to the high ground in I.27. and I.28.
6. ASSEMBLY. The Battalion will be ready to move off at 8.30 p.m. to-night in the following order :-
       "C", "D", "B", and "A" Coy's.   H.Qrs.
7. ROUTE. By Infantry Track through H.10. central then through H.17.a. to track in 17.d.4.5. then by track to railway at H.21.b.6.8. to positions in I.13. central.
       "C" Coy. on the right front.   "D" Coy. on the left.
       "B" behind "C".   "A" behind "D".
8. GUIDES. One Officer and one N.C.O. per Company have been shewn the position and the route, by 2/Lieut. L.J.Hobson this afternoon.
9. At zero hour the Battalion will move forward in Artillery formation to about I.21.a. central astride the road, where Companies will dig in if no cover is available, in the same order as in assembly positions.
   Zero hour will be notified later, but will be about 5 a.m. The signal for the Infantry to advance will be the opening of the barrage.
10. Lewis Guns will be carried on Limbers the whole way.

    ACKNOWLEDGE.
                         (sd) A.H.O. Riddell
                                                    Capt. & Adjt.
                              1st. Battalion Bedfordshire Regiment.

Copies to :-
1. O.C. "A" Coy.
2. "   "B" "
3. "   "C" "
4. "   "D" "
5. T.O.
6. R.S.M.
7. File.
8, 9, and 10.   War Diary.

S E C R E T.   O P E R A T I O N   O R D E R   No. 165.   Copy No. 10.

1st. Battalion The Bedfordshire Regiment.

Ref. — France 57.B. Scale 1/40,000.   Sept. 4th. 1918.

1. The Battalion will march to-day to the area H.19. and 20.
2. Order of march — H.Q., "A", "B", "C" and "D" Coy's. Transport.
   H.Q. to start off at 3.15 p.m. 100 yards interval to be maintained
   between Companies.
3. ROUTE. I.29.b. along road to FREMICOURT, by track to H.24.b.5.8.,
   along track to FAVREUIL, thence to monument at H.15.c.4.6. where guides
   will meet the Battalion.
4. Officers Valises, Mess Boxes etc., will be rolled and carried on haversacks.
5. Great Coats will be ready at 2 p.m.
6. Steel Helmets will be worn.

ACKNOWLEDGE.

(sd) W.H.O.Kiddell

1st. Bn. Bedfordshire Regiment.   Capt. & Adjt.

Copies to :—
1. H.Q., 15th. Infy. Bde.
2. O.C. "A" Coy.
3. "   "B" "
4. "   "C" "
5. "   "D" "
6. T.O.
7. R.S.M.
8. File.
9, 10, and 11. War Diary.

SECRET.

OPERATION ORDER No. 195.
1st. Battalion The Bedfordshire Regiment.

Ref. Map :- Sheet 57.C. and 1/40,000.   Sept. 14th. 1916.

- The Battalion will move into Divisional Reserve at VILLERS-au-FLOS, to-morrow the 15th. inst.
- Battalion will form up on ground at back of Battalion Headquarters, ready to move off at 10 a.m.
- DRESS - Full marching order. Caps to be worn.
- March discipline and the usual 200 yards interval between Companies will be maintained.
- ORDER OF MARCH. Headquarters, Drums, "A", "B", "C" and "D" Companies. Battalion will be clear of the Brigade Starting point (Fork roads at R.34.c.2.6.) by 11.30 a.m.
- ROUTE - BAPAUME - RIENCOURT - VILLERS-au-FLOS.
- Transport will march in rear of Battalion.
- Officers Kits, Mess Boxes, etc., will be stacked at Battalion H.Q., ready for loading by 9 a.m.
- Sgt. Foulder will superintend the loading of L.G. Limbers at 9 a.m.
- DUMPED Personnel will parade under Capt. J.C.A.Birch at Battalion H.Q. half an hour after departure of Battalion, when they will proceed to ACHIET le GRAND, and report to O.C., Divisional Reception Camp.
- Dumped Officers Kits will be ready for collection by Lorry on road opposite Transport Lines by 9 a.m.

H.H.(signature) 2/Lieut. & Adjt.
1st. Bn. Bedfordshire Regiment.

Copies to :-
1. Bde. H.Q.
2. C.O.
3. O.C. "A" Coy.
4. "   "B" "
5. "   "C" "
6. "   "D" "
7. T.O.
8. Q.M.
9. R.S.M.
10. Files.
11.)
12.) War Diary.
13.)

SECRET.   Copy No.
          O P E R A T I O N   O R D E R   No. 16b

                1st. Battalion The Bedfordshire Regiment.
                                                    Sept. 20th. 1918.

1. On the evening of the 20th. inst. the 1st. Battalion Bedfordshire Regt.
   will move into Support and take over from the 1st. D.C.L.I. in YTRES.
2. The Battalion will move in the following order :-
           H.Q., "B", "C", "D" and "A" Coy's. Transport.
   200 yards between Companies. Head of H.Q. to pass Church at VILLERS
   au FLOS at 5 p.m.
3. ROUTE - BARASTRE - BUS - YTRES.
4. DRESS - Full Marching order, with Steel Helmets on packs.
5. Billetting parties will take over details of working parties etc.,
   from 1st. D.C.L.I.
6. Officers Kits, Mess Boxes, etc., to be outside Coy. H.Q. at 3 p.m.
   Transport Officer will arrange to collect these.
7. Lewis Guns will be carried on Limbers in rear of each Coy.
8. Sgt. Washington will arrange for teas at 3.30 a.m.
9. Coy. Commanders to report to Battalion Headquarters when all their Coy
   is in Billets.

ACKNOWLEDGE.

                                                    Capt. & Adjt.
                1st. Battalion Bedfordshire Regiment.

NOTES ON ENEMY TRENCHES AND TERRITORY OPPOSITE IV CORPS FRONT.

(From Air Photographs only)

1. **HINDENBURG LINE.**
   (a) Trenches. The front and support trenches of the front line system from K 35 to BANTEUX, and the outpost line (PLUSH TRENCH) from K 35 to R 1) are in fairly good condition. The trenches have the appearance of having been cleared out and improved at many points at a comparatively recent date, but practically no new work has been noticeable during the past fortnight.

   (b) Wire. In K 35 & 36 the wire is not very strong and there are a number of gaps in front of both front and support trenches. The wire in front of PLUSH TRENCH is generally weak.

   In L 32 c & d the wire is fairly strong in places and grass has grown thickly amongst it (especially in front of VALLEY SUPPORT in L 31 c) There are gaps through wire in front of both trenches. It is damaged by shell fire where trenches cross road in L 31 d.

   In L 32 c wire appears weak in front of RIDGE SUPPORT and there are many gaps.

   In R 1 b wire in front of RIDGE TRENCH fairly strong in most places, but a few gaps.

   In R 2 a & b there are four strong belts, partially overgrown, in front of the front line, and three belts in front of WOOD SUPPORT west of the wood.

   In R 3 c wire is still fairly good but overgrown.

   There is very little wire in R 9 b & d.

   In R 16, 23, 29 & 30 wire is in good condition and is partially overgrown. There is a gap at R 23 c 10.75.

2. **TRENCHES AND WIRE ON LEFT DIVISIONAL FRONT.** (Other than HINDENBURG LINE)
   Trenches in Q 5,11,12, R 7 & 8 are all in fairly good condition. Practically no new work has been done either on the trenches or dug-outs.

   The wire is almost entirely our old wire and is consequently behind the trenches. It is mostly thin. Practically nothing has been done in the way of putting up wire in front of trenches (as now held by the enemy).

3. **TRENCHES AND WIRE ON RIGHT DIVISIONAL FRONT.**
   The same general remarks as in 2 (above) apply.
   Q 17 INKRAVEN TRENCH (in Q 17 b) in bad condition. No wire visible.
   Q 18 Trenches fair; wire thin.
   Q 23   do   do   Footbridge over trench at
                                           Q 23 d 85.35.
   Q 24 LINCOLN RESERVE & MIDLAND RESERVE in fairly good condition but wire thin.
   Q 29 AFRICAN TRENCH fair; wire weak.
   Q 30 Trench in Q 30 a & c fair; no wire.
   R 13,19,25. Trenches fair; wire very weak.
   R 14 Trenches and wire in fair condition; no trenches have been cleared out or worked upon.
   R 20 Trenches fairly good; wire thin.
   R 26 Trenches have fallen-in in places and no attempt at repair has been made; wire fairly strong.
   R 15 Trenches in very bad condition; wire still fairly strong, but numerous gaps.
   R 21 Trenches and wire fairly good.
   R 27 Trenches poor; gaps in wire at R 27 a 3.2; general condition of wire fair.

Notes on Enemy Trenches etc.   (2)

4. ROADS.

TRESCAULT - RIBECOURT   In good repair. Both craters in K 36 c have been filled in.

BEAUCAMP - K 36 c 0.1.   Out of use and very rough. Probably impassible except just N.E. of BEAUCAMP. The road is sunken and forms a defensive line. There are dug-outs in the bank at BOAR COPSE and at Q 6 a 15.55.

BEAUCAMP - RIBECOURT   In fair repair, but narrow. There is a crater at K 36 d 8.0, but road has been made around it. From PLUSH TRENCH Northwards the road is sunken, but trenches do not cut it. Fit for horse transport.

VILLERS-PLOUICH - RIBECOURT   In moderate repair. The road is fairly narrow and is sunken in L 31. It crosses all trenches. It is damaged by shell fire in L 31 b & d. Fit for horse transport.

BEAUCAMP North along HIGHLAND RIDGE. Not in use and impassible. Cut by trenches.

VILLERS-PLOUICH - MARCOING In use and in good repair.
MARCOING through COUILLET WOOD   do   do
COUILLET WOOD - RIBECOURT Fair condition; not cut by trenches. Fit for horse transport.

BEAUCAMP - VILLERS-PLOUICH Fair condition, except midway between villages. Crosses all trenches. Fit for horse transport.

Q 23 b to VILLERS-PLOUICH Bad condition.
Q 23 b to GOUZEAUCOURT Fairly good repair.
GOUZEAUCOURT - BOIS LATEAU Good repair; much used.
GOUZEAUCOURT - VILLERS-PLOUICH Fairly good condition.
GOUZEAUCOURT - LA VACQUERIE (VILLAGE ROAD) Fairly good repair and much used.
   do   do   (WELSH ROAD) Not in use; impassible.
VILLERS-PLOUICH - GONNELIEU Good repair.
ROADS IN L 34.   Poor and out of use. Impassible in places.

5. RAILWAY.

The MARCOING - VILLERS-PLOUICH - GOUZEAUCOURT line is in good repair as far South as VILLERS-PLOUICH, but immediately South of this it is damaged by shell fire. There are several craters along the line (probably wilful demolition). These have been there for more than two weeks.

6. COUILLET WOOD.

Consists almost entirely of thick undergrowth. There are very few trees. Trenches in the wood are in good condition and the belts of wire in front of the trenches are continuous except where cut by the road.

Branch Intelligence Section.
IV CORPS. 23:9:1918.

1st Bedfords

SECRET.   5th Divn No. O.C./672

STANDING ADMINISTRATIVE INSTRUCTIONS FOR BATTLE.

1. DUMPED PERSONNEL.
(a) Brigades will be responsible that correct numbers are kept up. Changes of Officers or Other Ranks may be made on Brigade authority.
(b) Dumped personnel will rejoin Brigades, if demanded, on Brigades coming into Divisional Reserve. Orders for these moves will be sent direct by Brigades to O.C., Dumped Personnel at the Reception Camp.
(c) Surplus to dumped personnel, both Officers and Other Ranks, i.e., returning leave parties - not originally counted as dump, casuals and reinforcements will be sent up automatically every day whenever Brigades are in Support or Reserve, and may be sent up on demand of Brigades on Reception Camp when Brigades are in the line.

2. SUPPLY. Men taking part in operations will always start with one days complete rations, plus the iron ration. When necessary, a double refill will be made under Divisional orders

3. TRANSPORT.
(a) During active operations, or when specially ordered in trench warfare, baggage wagons will remain with units, but the horses and drivers will return to the Train Companies. On move days, Brigades will demand direct on Train Company concerned for the horses and drivers. When the Division goes into Reserve on completion of move, baggage wagons will revert to the Train Companies.
(b) Formation of "A" and "B" Echelons. These will be formed for all active operations, but the Division will not take over control of "B" Echelons unless an advance of considerable depth is anticipated.

4. DRESS.
(a) Packs may be worn in fighting order instead of the haversack, at discretion of B.Gs.C. Where this is done, the spare kit normally carried in the pack will be transferred to sandbags. Brigades are authorised to demand sandbags from the C.R.E. for this purpose. Each sandbag containing kit must have its owners name, number and unit clearly painted or marked with indelible pencil on the outside.
(b) Great coats when taken forward and then dumped prior to action must be secured in bundles with the number of Platoon, Coy. and Unit on a label on each bundle. 10 or 12 coats is the most suitable number to form one bundle. Units will prepare necessary labels beforehand.
(c) Aeroplane Signalling Discs. 100 Discs per Battalion will be arranged and units will keep up this number under unit arrangements. Orders as to who wears them and where, will be issued by "G".

5. R.E. SERVICES. Tools, Tapes, sandbags, and other R.E. material required for operations will be obtained direct from R.E., by Brigades. Demands for any special tools, etc., for carriage on the man during operations will be repeated to this office.

6. AMMUNITION SUPPLY.
(a) All Infantry munitions will be demanded by Brigades direct on S.A.A. Section, D.A.O. If any special article is required demands will be repeated to this office. No dumps will be formed to replace mobile supply without authority from this office. The locations of all such authorised dumps will be reported to this office, and any changes in their contents reported.

P.T.O.

6. Cont'd.

(b) __Ammunition Supply by Aeroplane.__ Demands for ammunition to be so delivered will be sent by pigeon post or priority wire, addressed to 5th Division "Q" Advanced, and may be sent direct by unit concerned. An Aeroplane can drop 2 boxes at a time. This service is unreliable in windy weather.

(c) __S.A.A. Section, D.A.C.__ When the Division is in the line, or when the Artillery is detached from the Division, the S.A.A. Section is under control of "Q" Branch and moves and is quartered under orders issued by "Q". This takes effect from the receipt of orders to move into the line, or for the Artillery to be detached. The S.A.A. Section, D.A.C. reverts to control of C.R.A. when Division is in Reserve, to take effect from receipt of orders to move into Reserve, so that S.A.A. Section, D.A.C. will move out and be accommodated in Reserve by C.R.A.

7. __MEDICAL.__ When operations take place under conditions necessitating a long carry for Stretcher Bearers, the A.D.M.S. is allowed up to 20 Bearers per Infantry Brigade, to assist. Authority will be given in Administrative Instructions for each operation.

8. __PROVOST DUTIES.__ Divl. Employ. Coy. will, during extensive operations, detail a guard of one Officer, 3 N.C.O's and 15 men, for guard on Prisoners-of-War cage, and escorts over short distances. The D.A.P.M. will demand on D.E.C. for this guard on receipt of orders for any extensive operations.

9. __BURIAL PARTY.__ This party will normally commence work up to captured area on Z plus 1 day. The S.A.A. Section, D.A.C. will hold one G.S. Wagon available for use of this party on Z plus 1 day and onwards during all operations.

10. __SALVAGE.__ The O.C. Train will hold one G.S. Wagon available for movement of Salvage Company on Z plus 1 and subsequent days of any operations.

11. __ACKNOWLEDGE.__

                                        (signed) White
                                        Lt.Colonel,
23/9/1918.   A.A. & Q.M.G., 5th Division.

Copies to:—

13th Inf. Bde.	95th Inf. Bde.	15th Inf. Bde.
C.R.A.	C.R.E.	A.D.M.S.
5th Div. Train.	5th Signal Coy.	D.A.D.O.S.
D.A.P.M.	1/5th A.&.S.Hrs.	5th Bn. M.G.C.
208th D.E.C.	5th Div. "G".	Salvage Officer.
Burial Officer.	Div. Reception Camp.	

5th Division I.C.

INFORMATION FROM AEROPLANE PHOTOGRAPHS.

A. TRENCHES.

1. A continuation has been added at Q.13.a.3/5 and this trench now runs North as far as the VILLERS-PLOUICH - BEAUCAMP Road (59 L.B. 1016 and 59 L.B. 1018).

2. The trench shown on the Map as being in the Sunken Road west of RHONDDA POST (R.7.d.) is depicted about 100 yds. E. of this Road, on the photograph (59.L.B. 1006).

3. New work appears in TAFF VALE AVENUE between R.13.a.85/40 and 95/55. The remainder of this trench as far as R.13.b.05/92 seems disused and in a bad state of repair (59.L.B.997).

4. 6 fire-bays and a short length of trench appear to have been constructed in the disused trench from Q.18.d.20/05 to Q.24.b.02/85 (59.L.B. 999.).

5. A second fire-bay has been added to the S. side of the trench at Q.24.b.19/83. In appearance this fire-bay is similar to that already constructed on the N. side of the trench (59.L.B. 999).

6. NEW YEAR TRENCH and DICK AVENUE (R.14.a.) appear disused and in a bad state of repair. (59.L.B. 924.)

7. POPE AVENUE (R.14.central) seems disused in the vicinity of R.14.c.75/90 (59.L.B.924.)

8. The trench running immediately N. of, and parallel to, DUNRAVEN TRENCH in Q.18.a. and 17.b. has apparently been obliterated about Q.17.b.9/6 (59.L.B.959.)

B. TRACKS.

1. A well defined and apparently much used track is shewn running from Q.18.d.2/5. EASTWARDS as far as R.13.c.10/55.

2. Two are shewn leading WEST from DUNRAVEN TRENCH at R.19.a.5/6.
The Northern one runs along the NORTH side of the Sunken Road to the bank at Q.24.b.65/75. The Southern one runs along the SOUTH side of the Sunken Road, and North of the track indicated on the Map, in the general direction of LINCOLN RESERVE. There are numerous paths along the South side of the bank from Q.24.b.2/6 to R.19.a.0/8 (59.L.B.999.)

3. Two tracks are shewn leading out S.W. from VILLERS PLOUICH. One from R.13.d.15/39 through R.13.c.0/7 to Q.18.d.05/40. The second from R.13.d.15/39 to R.19.a.20/65, where it probably links up with the tracks given in para 2 above. (59.L.B. 1016.)

4. Tracks radiate S. and S.E. from R.13.b.2/3. One runs parallel to the VILLERS PLOUICH - GOUZEAUCOURT ROAD and two others join this road at R.13.b.35/20 and R.13.b.35/10 respectively. These have probably been brought into use to divert traffic proceeding S. from the main road junction at R.13.b.35/25. (59.L.B. 997.)

2.

5. A track is indicated running almost parallel to the TRIG POST - VILLERS PLOUICH ROAD from Q.18.d.0/4 to Q.23.b.9/2. The road itself is practically indistinguishable.(59. L.B. 1002).

6. From immediately N. of DURNFORD POST (Q.24.b.) a track leads S.W. to the road at Q.24.c.2/7 (59.L.B.1010).

7. From SURREY ROAD at R.14.b.15/70 a track leads along the gulley N.W. to the Road at R.8.c.63/30. (59.L.B.924.)

8. There are numerous paths in the vicinity of the junction of NAVAL RESERVE and FARM AVENUE (R.15.a.) A track is also visible from this junction running N.W. and parallel to MOUNTAIN ASH TRENCH, as far the road at R.8.c.9/8. (59.L.B. 924).

INTELLIGENCE.

24th September 1918.   5th Division.

SECRET.

Copy No. 13

15th Infantry Brigade Operation Order, No. 220.

24th September, 1918.

Reference :- Sheet, 57.c., S.E., Scale 1/20,000.

1. On the night of the 25th/26th September, 1918, the 95th Infantry Brigade will be relieved by the 13th and 15th Infantry Brigades in the Line.

2. The 15th Infantry Brigade will take over that portion of the Divisional Front from the junction of SNAP TRENCH with SOOT AVENUE, (exclusive), to the Northern Divisional Boundary with the 1st CHESHIRE Regiment.

3. The 1st CHESHIRE Regiment will relieve the 1st D.C.L.I., with Headquarters at QUARRY, (Q.16.c.2/2).
   One Company, 1st NORFOLK Regiment will be attached to the 1st CHESHIRE Regiment and will relieve the Left Company of the 1st DEVON Regiment.

4. 1st NORFOLK Regiment, (less one Company), will be in Support in their present line to North of Road in P.30.a., with Headquarters at Q.20.d.4/1., (at present Battalion Headquarters of the 12th GLOUCESTER Regiment).

5. 1st BEDFORDSHIRE and 16th R.WARWICKSHIRE Regiments will remain in their present positions.

6. 15th Trench Mortar Battery will relieve all guns of the 95th Trench Mortar Battery in position within the area detailed in para. 2.

7. All details of reliefs will be arranged between Commanding Officers concerned.
   No troops of relieving Battalions will pass East of the Grid Line dividing Squares P and Q before 7-0 p.m. 1st CHESHIRE Regiment will move up by tracks to South of METZ. Route to be thoroughly reconnoitred.

8. Completion of reliefs will be reported to Brigade Headquarters. Code word - name of Commanding Officer.

9. 15th Infantry Brigade Headquarters will close at YTRES at 8-0 p.m. will will re-open at BATTERY POST, (Q.22.a.5/3), at the same hour.

10. The Brigadier-General Commanding 15th Infantry Brigade will assume command of the Sector at 9-0 p.m.

A C K N O W L E D G E.

Issued at 2-30 p.m.

24th September, 1918.

Captain,
Brigade Major, 15th Infantry Brigade.

Copies to :- No. 1. B.G.C.   No. 2. Brigade Major.
              3. Staff Captain.   4. Intelligence Officer.
              5. Signal Officer.   6. Transport Officer.
              7. 5th Division, "G".   8. 5th Division, "Q".
              9. 13th Infy. Bde.   10. 95th Infy. Bde.
              11. Right Brigade,   12. 1st Norfolks.
                  (42nd Division).   14. 1st Cheshires.
              13. 1st Bedfords.   16. "C" Coy., 5th M.G.Bn.
              15. 16th R.Warwicks.   18. 15th T.M.Battery.
              17. 59th Field Coy.,R.E. 20. C.R.A., 5th Division.
              19. C.R.E., 5th Division. 22. 5th Battalion, M. Corps.
              21. No. 4 Coy., A.S.C.   24. Brigade Supply Officer.
              23. 15th Field Ambulance. 26. War Diary.
              25. War Diary.   27. Office Copy.

SECRET.  15th Infantry Brigade O.O. No. 221/1.

Addendum to 15th Infantry Brigade O.O. No. 221.

1. Reference para. 5 - At Zero plus 152 minutes, the hour at which the artillery barrage opens, 1st BEDFORDS will advance from their assembly positions and close up to the barrage.
   At Zero plus 158 minutes the barrage will commence to move forward.

2. Reference para. 8 - (a). A halt of 12 minutes will be made on this line. Infantry will arrive on it at Zero plus 186 minutes and leave at Zero plus 198 minutes.
   (b). A halt of eight minutes will be made on the Red Line. 1st BEDFORDS will arrive on it at Zero plus 222 minutes and 16th R.WARWICKS will pass through to the Brown Dotted Line at Zero plus 230 minutes.

   Barrage Maps are forwarded to 1st BEDFORDS, 1st CHESHIRES, 16th R.WARWICKS and "C" Company, 5th Machine Gun Battalion.

3. At Zero plus 152 minutes, burning oil drums will be projected opposite the Divisional Front of Attack.

25th September, 1918.   Brigade Major, 15th Infantry Brigade.
Captain,

Copies to :- All recipients
of 15th Infy. Bde. O.O. No. 221.

SECRET.   5th Division S.70/65.

....

In connection with the forthcoming attack the Major-General wishes to impress the following points on all Commanders.

COMMUNICATIONS.

It is essential that early and accurate knowledge should be obtained concerning the movement of troops on our flanks especially for Officers who are directing the operations.

On cannot rely upon the telephone and it is therefore necessary that Brigadiers and Commanding Officers should use as many alternative methods as possible.

(a) Liaison Officers should be established with flank battalions.
(b) Mounted Staff Officers should be employed as much as possible in obtaining information first-hand.
(c) Runner Posts should be established and if the distance exceeds 1,000 yards, relay posts must also be established.
(d). Runners with messages should be employed in pairs.
(e). Every runner should know the contents of the message and should be in a position to impart information verbally.
(f). Officers who are concerned in the actual fighting have a right to read and to obtain from runners all information which may be necessary to assist them in directing operations.
(g). NIL reports are valuable.
(h). If no information is obtainable it may be necessary for senior Officers to go up themselves and see for themselves what the situation is and personally direct subsequent operations.

2. Arrangements must be made that the Contact Aeroplanes can be shown either by flares or by discs the position of our most forward troops.

3. STOKES Mortars are invaluable for destroying nests of machine guns and full use should be made of their mobility and rapidity of fire both in the initial bombardment and subsequently in overcoming strong points and machine gun nests.

4. Special attention must be paid to "Mopping-up" and units must be detailed especially for this work. It is likely that in the Sunken Roads we have to pass over there will be many deep dug-outs and these will either have to be cleared or sentries posted over them.

In trenches blocks must be invariably made on our flanks.

It must be strongly impressed on all Platoon Commanders that "Crowding" or "Bunching" leads to many casualties.

In moving warfare and especially in the pursuit of an enemy Platoon Commanders must organise their Platoons with scouts in front and scouts on both flanks.

Advances should be made by bounds and platoons should not be allowed to wander off into the blue.

When Platoons or Companies are held up on their flanks the Platoons that are held up should still push forward and not

2.

their
wait on each other, but on/arrival at their objective, or on reaching the limit of the bound the Platoon Commander should think out some plan whereby he can deal with the enemy that is opposing the advance on his flanks.

G.W.Gordon Hull
Lieutenant-Colonel,
25th September 1918. General Staff, 5th Division.

Distribution down to Companies.

✱✱✱✱✱✱✱✱✱
S E C R E T .
✱✱✱✱✱✱✱✱✱

Copy No. 10

15th Infantry Brigade Operation Order, No. 221.

25th September, 1918.

Reference :- Sheet, 57.c., S.E., Scale 1/20,000.

1. On a date to be notified later, the offensive will be resumed by the Third Army.
    The IV Corps will attack with the 5th Division on the Right and the 42nd Division on the Left.
    The 17th Division, (V Corps), will attack on the right of the 5th Division.

2. The 5th Division will attack on a two Brigade Front, with the 13th Infantry Brigade on the Right and the 15th Infantry Brigade on the Left.
    The objectives and boundaries of the 15th Infantry Brigade are as shewn on the map issued to units of the 15th Infantry Brigade and 'A' Company, 11th Tank Battalion only.
    The objective of the 13th Infantry Brigade will be the Red Line within their Brigade boundaries.
    The final objective of the 42nd Division will be the Blue Line.

3. PLAN OF ATTACK.
    (a). 1st BEDFORDS will advance to the attack on a two Company front, one Company in Support and one in Reserve, and capture the Red objective. One Company will proceed to mop up the Western portion of BEAUCAMP.
    (b). 16th R.WARWICKS will follow behind 1st BEDFORDS and, during the halt ~~of 30 minutes~~ on Red objective, will close up on 1st BEDFORDS and be ready to go through to the Brown Dotted Line. The greatest care must be taken to dispose one Company to look after the Northern slope of the spur, as it is probable our attack will be slightly in advance of the Division on our ~~Right~~ Left.
    (c). 1st CHESHIRES will advance one Company from their position of assembly. Its role will be that of connecting link between the 1st BEDFORDS' Left and the Right of the 42nd Division, and thereafter the mopping up of the BEAUCAMP Valley and the Western and Northern portion of BEAUCAMP Village. The remaining three Companies will remain holding front and support trenches and will move under orders of Brigade Headquarters.
    (d). 1st NORFOLKS will remain in their assembly position in Reserve ready to move forward under orders of Brigade Headquarters.
    (e). The Light Trench Mortar Battery will assemble three guns with each leading Battalion and move forward with them taking on machine gun nests during the advance. Covering fire is to be given on every possible target over the heads of advancing Infantry and the guns must be pushed well forward. Two guns will remain in reserve ready to move forward at very short notice.
    (f). "C" Company, Machine Gun Battalion are allotted the following tasks :-
        (i). Two sections will come into action about Q.18.b.4/5 and sweep the Valley to VILLERS PLOUICH and the BEAUCAMP Spur, giving covering fire to the advance of the 16th R.WARWICKS.
        (ii). One Section will advance with the 16th R.WARWICKS and come into action about R.7.b.1/7 and R.7.d.5/8, to sweep the Valley and assist in covering the advance of the 42nd Division on our Left to the Blue objective.
        (iii). One section will be kept in reserve.
    At every opportunity direct overhead covering fire is to be employed to assist the Infantry.

P.T.O.

(g). **Tanks.** One Section of "A" Company, 11th Tank Battalion, (Mark 5, ~~Stars~~ *Stars*), will operate on the Brigade Front.

The routes to be taken by Tanks are shewn on the attached tank track map. [Each tank will be accompanied by three men, who will form a smoke screen for them. After the Red objective is taken one tank will rally South of BEAUCAMP and two North of the Village] ready to advance to the Brown Dotted Line.

—[It must be impressed on Infantry that they are not to follow the Tanks but keep their direction assisting the Tanks on their asking for help in mopping up.

Signals are as follows :-

Tanks to Infantry :-
- White and Green Flag, ... Come to me.
- Red and Yellow Flag, ... Am out of action, go on without me.
- Red, Blue and White Flag, ... Am withdrawing, dont shoot.

Infantry to Tanks :-
- Helmet waved on rifle, ... Come to me.]—

4. It should be noted that the plan of attack aims at using the high ground as the line of advance in order to be above hostile machine guns, and also so as to be exposed to fire from the front and one flank only, instead of both flanks, and also to pinch out BEAUCAMP Valley and Village.

—[The directing point, if not obscured by mist and smoke, is the high tree South and East of BEAUCAMP Village, the true bearing of which is 35° from Q.23.a.90/15.

The true bearing of the line of advance of each Battalion will be taken.

Every Officer must carefully set his compass in case of fog or smoke obscuring the directing point.]—

5. The actual timings of the attack, and the hours of arrival on, and departure from, each objective for the attacking troops will be issued later.

6. LINE OF CONSOLIDATION.

1st BEDFORDS will consolidate in depth on a front from Q.18.a.9/1, (in touch with the 13th Infantry Brigade), along LINCOLN Reserve Trench as far as R.13.a.0/8, (Sunken Road).

16th R.WARWICKS from this point to RHONDDA Post - TRENT ALLEY: they must note the necessity of holding PLOUGH Trench until the 42nd Division come up into line, and then of gaining touch with the 42nd Division about R.7.b.9/0.

The strictest orders are to be issued that men are not to go into any dug-outs or shelters until they have been visited by the Tunnelling Section. Trenches even should not be occupied until a good inspection has been made; shell holes are preferable. Use should be made of prisoners to find out whether trenches are mined.

7. ASSEMBLY.

Assembly positions are shewn on the attached map. A short length of trench will be dug by a Support Company of 1st CHESHIRES on Y/Z night from Q.22.b.8/4 to Q.22.b.7/7, (orders for this will be issued separately), for the use of 16th R.WARWICKS.

Route of assembly on Y/Z night will be WINCHESTER Valley Track - QUIVERING Support and QUOTIENT Trenches to BANK Post, thence along Communication Trench to TRIG Post.

Rear of 1st BEDFORDS to be clear of CEMETERY, (P.23.c.5/4), by 9-0 p.m. 16th R.WARWICKS will follow 500 yards in rear. Platoons to move at 150 yards interval.

Track will be carefully reconnoitred by 1st BEDFORDS and 16th R.WARWICKS. In addition, directing control posts will be placed by the Brigade Staff.

Before dawn the camouflage provided will be placed in position w... down into the trench leaving just sufficient room for the troops to lie under.

When the 1st BEDFORDS and 16th R.WARWICKS arrive in position the Company of the 1st NORFOLKS holding the line will rejoin its battalion. The remainder of the line will continue to be held as at present by the 1st CHESHIRES.

8. ARTILLERY.

The attack will be carried out under a barrage which creeps at the rate of 100 yards in four minutes with the following halts :-
   (a). On the line - Q.11.d.8/6 - Road at Q.11.d.9/3 - Road at Q.18.a.0/8 - trench at Q.18.a.4/4 - along line of trench to junction at Q.18.a.8/1 - LINCOLN RES at Q.18.d.0/6.
   (b). On the Red Line.
Actual duration of halts will be notified later.

9. MACHINE GUN BARRAGE.

One Company, Machine Gun Battalion, will fire a direct and indirect machine gun barrage. The guns firing direct will cover the gap, (200 yards), between 1st BEDFORDS' Left and 1st CHESHIRES' Right and the gap, (350 yards), between Left of 1st CHESHIRES and 42nd Division. This fire will be on a wide arc at first and gradually narrow down.

All ranks are to be informed that it is direct fire and that they can be seen by the firers. It will not take place in case of fog.

Machine Gun barrage, (one Company), is of the usual nature - 500 yards in front of advancing Infantry.

10. MEDIUM TRENCH MORTARS.

Medium trench mortars operating on the 15th Infantry Brigade Front of attack are grouped as follows :-
   Six to enfilade trenches in Q.17.b.
   Six to bombard BEAUCAMP.
   Twelve to enfilade trenches on BEAUCAMP Ridge or bombard trenches in Q.23.d.

11. SIGNALS.

   (a). On the capture of the Red Line two white lights will be sent up by the 1st BEDFORDS.
   (b). Red flares will be dropped by counter-attack patrol machines to denote that enemy are massing for counter-attack.
   (c). White ground flares will be lighted when called for by contact 'planes. Tin discs will also be used to shew our positions to contact aeroplanes.

12. HEADQUARTERS.

15th Infantry Brigade Headquarters will be at BATTERY POST, (Q.22.a.5/2), with advanced report centre and observation post at Q.23.a.9/2.

Headquarters of "C" Company, 5th Machine Gun Battalion, will be near Brigade Headquarters.

Battalion Headquarters will be established as follows on Y/Z night :-
   1st BEDFORDS,   ) Q.23.a.8/4.
   16th R.WARWICKS,)
   1st CHESHIRES,   QUARRY, Q.16.c.2/2.
   1st NORFOLKS,   Q.20.c.65/70.

Headquarters of 15th Trench Mortar Battery will be with 1st BEDFORDS.

13. ZERO HOUR.

Z Day and Zero Hour will be notified later.

Watches will be synchronized on Y/Z night under arrangements of the Brigade Signal Officer.

14. ACKNOWLEDGE.
****

Issued at 11-0 a.m.

25th September, 1918.

J.F. Stuart.
Captain,
Brigade Major, 15th Infantry Brigade.

P.T.O.

Copies to :- No. 1. B.G.C.
2. Brigade Major.
3. Staff Captain.
4. Intelligence Officer.
5. Signal Officer.
6. Transport Officer.
7. 5th Division, "G". * ≠
8. 5th Division, "Q".
9. 1st Norfolks. *
10. 1st Bedfords. * ✓
11. 1st Cheshires. *
12. 16th R.Warwicks. *
13. 15th T.M.Battery. *
14. 'C' Coy., 5th M.G.Bn. *
15. 59th Field Coy.,R.E.
16. 15th Field Ambulance.
17. 13th Infy. Bde
18. 95th Infy. Bde.
19. 125th Infy. Bde.
20. 126th Infy. Bde.
21. 'A' Coy.,11th Tank Bn. *
22. C.R.A., 5th Division.
23. A.D.M.S.
24. War Diary.
25. War Diary.
26. Office Copy.
----

* Denotes Maps attached.

≠ Map shewing assembly positions only attached.

App I

SECRET.   Copy No.

OPERATION ORDER No. 137.

1st. Battalion The Bedfordshire Regiment.

Map Ref. - 51 at 57.C. S.E.   Scale 1/20,000.

Sept. 28th. 1918.

---

1. On a date to be notified later the offensive will be resumed by the 3rd. Army.
   The IV Corps will attack with the 5th. Divn. on the right and the 42nd. Divn. on the left.
   The 17th. Divn. (V Corps) will attack on the right of the 5th. Division.
   The 5th. Division will attack on a two Brigade front, with the 13th. Infy. Bde. on the right and the 15th. Infy. Bde. on the left.

2. The 1st. Bedfordshire Regt. will capture the RED objective, from R.13.a. 0.8. (junction of trench and sunken road) to Q.18.K.9.1.
   The 16th. R.Warwicks will follow behind 1st. Bedfords, and go through to the BROWN dotted line, after the RED objective has been captured.
   The 1st. Cheshires will be in support, with one Coy. linking up left of 1st. Bedfords with the right of the 42nd. Divn. afterwards helping to mop up BEAUCAMP VALLEY.   1st. Norfolks will be in reserve.
   The objective of the 13th. Bde. will be the RED line within their Bde. boundaries.   The final objective of the 42nd. Divn. will be the BLUE line as shown on special map issued to Companies.

3. **PLAN OF ATTACK.**   "A" and "C" Coy's. will attack in the front line, "A" on the right and "C" on the left, each having two platoons in the front wave, and two in immediate support. 15 yards between lines and 50 yards between waves.   "D" Coy. will be in support, 100 yards distance in the same formation, two platoons supporting "A" Coy. and two supporting "C". "B" Coy. in reserve at 200 yards distance, in Artillery formation, with sections echeloned.
   As soon as the barrage lifts to the RED objective, "B" Coy. will proceed to mop up the Western portion of BEAUCAMP.   They will be assisted by one Tank.
   One section of Tanks will operate on the Brigade front, each Tank will be accompanied by three men, who will form a smoke screen for them.   After the RED objective is taken, one tank will rally South of BEAUCAMP, and two North of the village.
   It must be impressed on Infantry that they are not to follow the Tanks, but keep their direction Assisting the Tanks on the asking for help in mopping up.
   Signals are as follows :-

   Tanks to Infantry :-
   White and Green Flag   ...   ...   Come to me.
   Red and Yellow Flag   ...   ...   Am out of action. Go on without me.
   Red, Blue and White Flag ... ... Am withdrawing, Don't shoot.

   Infantry to Tanks :-
   Helmet waved on rifle ...   ...   Come to me.

4. The directing point, if not obscured by mist and smoke, is the high tree South and East of BEAUCAMP VILLAGE, the true bearing of which is 35 degrees from Q.23.a.90.15.
   The true bearing of the line of advance of each Battalion will be taken. Every Officer must carefully set his compass, in case of fog or smoke obscuring the directing point.

5. **CONSOLIDATION.**   The 1st. Bedfords will consolidate in depth, with "A" and "C" Coy's. in the front line, from Q.18.a.9.1. to R.13.a.0.8.   "B" Coy, after mopping up Village, will move into support at Q.18.a.6.6. to Q.12.d. 4.2.   "D" Coy. will withdraw to the neighbourhood of the sunken Road about Q.17.b.6.0. to Q.18.a.2.6, with Battalion Headquarters in the sunken Road about Q.17.b.5.2.

No dug-outs or shelters are to be entered in captured trenches, until they have been visited by the Tunnelling section. Use should be made of prisoners to find out whether the trenches are mined.

6. **ASSEMBLY.** Battalion will move to assembly positions which have been allotted to Companies on Y/Z night.
ROUTE of assembly will be WINCHESTER VALLEY TRACK — WOLVERINE Support and WOLLENT Trenches to BARK POST, thence along communication trench to FRED POST.
Order of march — "C", "B", "D" and "A" Coy's. H.Q. 150 yards interval between platoons. Rear of H.Q. to pass Cemetery (R.25.c.5.d.) by 9 p.m.
Time of start will be notified later.
Battalion Headquarters will be at Q.27.a.8.d.

7. **ARTILLERY.** The attack will be carried out under a barrage which creeps at the rate of 100 yards in 4 minutes, with the following halts :—
(a) On the line — Q.11.d.8.8. — Road at Q.11.b.9.3. — Road at Q.18.a.9.8. — Trench at Q.18.a.4.6. — along line of trench to Junction at Q.18.a.6.1. — LIBCOLN ROAD at Q.18.d.9.3.
(b) On the RED Line.
Actual duration of halts will be notified later.

8. **MACHINE GUN BARRAGE.** One Coy. M.G. Battalion will fire a direct and indirect machine gun barrage. The guns firing direct will cover the gap (500 yards) between 1st. Bedfords left and 1st. Cheshires right, and the gap (850 yards) between left of 1st. Cheshires and 42nd. Divn. This fire will be on a wide arc at first, and gradually narrow down.
All ranks are to be informed that it is direct fire, and that they can be seen by the firers. It will not take place in case of fog.
Machine gun barrage (One Coy) is of the usual nature, — 500 yards in front of advancing Infantry.

9. **MEDIUM TRENCH MORTARS.** Medium Trench Mortars operating on the 15th. Infantry Bde. front of attack are grouped as follows :—
6 to enfilade trenches in Q.17.b.
6 to bombard BEAUCAMP.
12 to enfilade trenches on BEAUCAMP RIDGE or bombard trenches in Q.21.d.

10. **SIGNALS.** (a) On the capture of the RED Line, two white lights will be sent up by the 1st. Bedfords.
(b) Red flares will be dropped by Counter attack patrol machines to denote that enemy are massing for counter attack.
(c) White ground flares will be lighted when called for by Contact Planes. Tin Discs will also be used to show our positions to Contact Aeroplanes.

11. **ZERO HOUR.** "Z" Day and Zero hour will be notified later.
Watches will be synchronised on Y/Z night under arrangements of the Intelligence Officer.

12. **STORES.** Stores to be carried will be issued to Companies on "Y" Day.

Hot tea will be issued at midnight on Y/Z night, and breakfast provided on Z Day.

Companies will report to Battalion Headquarters by name of Coy. Commander when Companies are in assembly positions.

ACKNOWLEDGE.

R.N.O. Riddell Capt. & Adjt.
1st. Battalion The Bedfordshire Regiment.

Copies to :—
1. H.Q., 15th. Infy. Bde.   8. R.S.M.
2 to 5. O.C. Coy's.   9. File.
6. Q.M.   10, 11 and 12. War Diary.
7. T.O.

SECRET. COPY NO.- 4

OPERATION ORDER No. 148.
1st BATTALION THE CHESHIRE REGIMENT.
IN THE FIELD. 26/9/18.

Reference Map:- Sheet 57.c., S.E. 1/20,000.

1. On Z day the 15th Infantry Brigade will attack in conjunction with the 13th Infantry Brigade on right, and the 42nd Division on the left.
   The 1st BEDFORDS will advance at Zero plus 152 minutes and will capture the Red objective between BARD LANE Q.18.b.2.3. and YORK AVENUE at Q.12.b.3.0. They will reach this line at Zero plus 222 minutes. One Company will be detached to mop up the Western portion of BEAUCAMP.
   The 16th R. WARWICKS will follow behind 1st BEDFORDS and during the halt on Red objective will close up and be ready to go through to the Brown Dotted Line, which will be the second objective, at Zero plus 230 minutes.
   These Battalions will consolidate as under:
   1st BEDFORDS from Q.18.a.9.1. along LINCOLN RESERVE Trench as far as R.13.a.0.8. (Sunken Road).
   16th R. WARWICKS from this point to RHONDDA Post - TRENT ALLEY, and will gain touch with the 42nd Division about R.7.b.9.0.

2. "A" Company, 1st CHESHIRES, will take up Fire Positions along SNAP Trench between Railway at Q.17.c.8.7. and Road at Q.17.a.3.1. and will, when the advance begins, open a barrage of grazing fire and L.G. fire in the direction of the S.W. Corner of BEAUCAMP Village at Q.12.c.2.0. covering the gap between the 1st BEDFORDS and "B" Company, 1st CHESHIRES. This fire will be discontinued as soon as the advancing troops can no longer be kept in view. "A" Company will remain in the fire trench and will be under the orders of the Battalion Commander.
   "B" Company will assemble in SNAP Trench between Q.17.a.3.4. and Trench junction Q.17.a.2.8. and will, at Zero plus 152 minutes, advance as a connecting link between the 1st BEDFORDS and the Right of the 42nd Division, and thereafter will mop up BEAUCAMP Valley and the Western and Northern portion of BEAUCAMP Village. The True Bearing of this advance will be about 70°. Their Right flank will include CHARING CROSS and the Sunken Road running N.E. from CHARING CROSS to Q.11.d.5.0. Two sections will be detached to work along DUNRAVEN Support towards flank of 1st BEDFORDS advance. On completion of task "B" Company will assemble and re-organise W. of BEAUCAMP Village about Q.12.c.2.3.
   "C" and "D" Companies will remain in reserve about Q.16.a.1.6. and Q.16.a.0.4. respectively, but will be ready to move forward and occupy or advance from Fire Trenches at a moments notice.

3. ARTILLERY barrage opens at Zero plus 152 minutes. At Zero plus 158 minutes barrage will creep forward at 100 yds in four minutes with the following halts:-
   (a) On the line
       Q.11.d.8.6. - Road at Q.11.d.9.3. - Road at Q.13.a.0.8.
       12 minutes halt.
   Infantry will reach this line at Zero plus 186 minutes.
   (b) On the Red Line - 8 minutes halt.
       1st BEDFORDS will reach this line at Zero plus 222 minutes.
   At Zero plus 152 minutes burning oil drums will be projected opposite the front.

4. MACHINE GUNS.
   One Company, M.G.s will fire
   (a) indirect barrage 500 yds in front of the advancing troops
   (b) direct fire to cover the gaps (200 yds) between 1st BEDFORDS left and "B" Company, 1st CHESHIRES, right, and the gap (250 yds) between left of 1st CHESHIRES and 42nd Division.
   This fire will be on a wide arc at first and gradually die down.
   All ranks are to be informed that it is direct fire and that they can be seen by the firers.

5. MEDIUM TRENCH MORTARS.
   6 Medium Trench Mortars will enfilade the trenches in Q.17.b.
   6 will bombard BEAUCAMP.

6. TANKS will co-operate in the attack. It must, however, be impressed on all ranks that they are not to follow the tanks but must

P.T.O./keep.

- 2 -

keep their direction assisting the Tanks on their asking for help in mopping up. All ranks must be made acquainted with the Tank Signals.

Tank Tracks:-
No.1 - Q.17.d.5.0. to Q.18.a.6.0. to Q.18.a.0.5. to Q.18.b.5.9.;
No.2 - Q.17.a.6.0. to Q.17.b.2.2. to Q.18.a.4.3. then through BEAUCAMP to Q.12.c.9.7.
No.3 - Q.11.c.3.2. along North side of BEAUCAMP.

7. SIGNALS.
On the capture of the Red Line two white lights will be sent up by the 1st BEDFORDS.

8. ENEMY MINES.
Men are to be warned not to go into any dug-out until it has been visited by the Tunnelling Section. Even Trenches should be occupied with caution. Prisoners should be questioned as to presence of mines.

9. PRISONERS will be sent back under escort of slightly wounded men to the Sunken Road by Regtl. Aid Post in Q.16.c.2.6. No unwounded man should be sent back for this purpose.

10. REGIMENTAL AID POST will be in Sunken Road Q.16.c.4.6.

11. Battalion H.Q. will be in QUARRY in Q.16.c.2.2.
A Forward observing station and report centre will be established by Left Company H.Q. at Q.11.c.4.2.

12. ZERO HOUR will be notified later.

13. COMPASSES will be set.

14. WATCHES will be synchronised on Y/Z night at a time to be notified later.

15. A C K N O W L E D G E   IN WRITING.

ISSUED AT 11 a.m.

Captain and Adjutant,
1st Battalion the Cheshire Regiment.

COPIES TO:-

1. 15th Inf. Bde.
2. C.O.
3. Major H.S. WALKER.
4. O.C., 1st BEDFORDS.
5. O.C. "A" Coy.
6. O.C. "B" Coy.
7. O.C. "C" Coy.
8. O.C. "D" Coy.
9. I.O.
10. M.O.
11. L.G.O.
12. Q.M.
13. T.O.
14. R.S.M.
15. War Diary.
16. War Diary.
17. Retained.

5th Infy. Bde. N° G.A.1.

1/Bedfords/
16/R.War.R

1. Ref. para 7 of O.O. N° 221 –

Head of Bedfords will be at Cemetery (P.23.c.5/4) at 8 pm & will be clear of it by 9 pm.

Head of 16th R.War.R. to be at Cemetery at 9-15 pm.

Directing posts of 1st Norfolks will be placed along the track in pairs at intervals of 250 yards from about Q.25.a. 9/7 to Bde. H.Q. at BATTERY Post.

Company markers for the assembly positions will be sent up in advance in parties of 2 or 3 & may be put in position in daylight.

2. Unless orders to the contrary are received the move to assembly positions will take place today, 26th Sept.

26/9/18.

J.Stuart
CAPTAIN,
BRIGADE MAJOR.
15TH INFANTRY BRIGADE

Operation Archery

SECRET

A 9ot.
Passiquers   B HH.
               C R.S.
               3 Rfs.

15   Intelligence Report
                          6 a.m. 6th Oct. 1918

OPERATIONS

Our Artillery shelled BEAUCAMP and in rear of the
Village from 12.30 to 1.20 p.m. and from 2 to 2.10 p.m.
Hostile activity in the part of our aeroplanes from noon
till dark. At no night flying planes were active and no enemy
bombing planes were over.

PATROLS

One N.C.O. and 4 O.R's left DUNRAVEN TRENCH
(point Q.17a 7/6) at 1 a.m. to reconnoitre CHARING CROSS
and the road running S.E. from it. Two of the enemy
were seen walking West along the trench at about Q.17a 9/8
no further movement observed and patrol returned to Q.17a 7/6
at 2.40 a.m.

ENEMY ACTIVITY

MOVEMENT   Movement in the Sunken Road from Q.17d 5/-
to Q.12c 1/15 was above normal yesterday. The Hut, a dug-out
at Q.17d 5/4 and the smaller ones to the N.E. are still centres
of activity. During the day movement was seen at 16 different
places along this road which is apparently strongly held. All
groups were wearing steel helmets and equipment.
   Men observed walking in a hollow S.E of BEAUCAMP at 8 a.m.
During our daylight patrol activity, the enemy occupied
the SUNKEN ROAD apparently stood to, and 2 machine
guns opened fire from CHARING CROSS.

ARTILLERY   Front Line was shelled with 4.2's from
7 to 8 a.m. & from 8.45 to 10 a.m. 77 m.m fired
on Front Line at 12.45 p.m. and 5.9's at 2.15 a.m.
   SUPPORT COY'S positions shelled with 77 m.m at
11.15 a.m. and 2.30 p.m., and on Q.30 p.m with Gas Shells
(nature unreported). 'SNIP' LANE shelled with 77 m.m &
4.2's throughout the night, 77 m.m fired 5-minute
bursts on Q.22 d (N of GOUZEAUCOURT WOOD) at 9.5,
10.5 & 11.5 p.m. The QUARRY, TRESCAULT VALLEY &
Q.16 were shelled with H.E & gas intermittently throughout
the day & night as usual.

MACHINE GUNS.   During the relief a M.G. traversed
our R' Coy's lines — position as yet unlocated.

TRENCH MORTARS   L.T.M bombs were fired in vicinity
of Dead Man's Corner at about 8 p.m.

P.T.O

AEROPLANES   E.A. were over at 3.3 p.m., 3.20 p.m., 3.40 p.m.
and 5.50 p.m. — attitudes invariably approached.
Between 8.30 & 10 p.m. E.A. bombed WINCHESTER &
TRESCAULT villages.

GENERAL   8 a.m. green lights put up from ne corner of
BEAUCAMP — no result observed.

26th Sep. 1918   G P Platt
                                   Lt. I.O.
                                  15th Suf. Regt.

SECRET   Copy No. 2

15th Infy. Bde. O.O. No. 223.

29-9-1918.

1) At 4 am on 30th Sept., the advance will be continued by 15th Infy. Bde. in order to cover the right flank of the N.Z. Division who have reached R.17. central.

2) At 4 am a barrage will come down on a line 500 yards West of the Sunken Road running through R.21.d. & will dwell there for 5 minutes.

At 4-5 am it will commence to creep forward at 100 yards in 5 minutes with the following halts.

  10 minutes - on line of BARRACK TRENCH.

3) The advance will be carried out by 1st Cheshires in front who will be responsible for the capture of 1st objective - BARRACK TRENCH & SUPPORT.

The 1st Norfolks will follow in rear of 1st Cheshires & will pass through them on the 1st objective to the capture of the final objective -

  a line from R.28.b.2/2 - R.28.b.9/9, thence along Sunken Road to R.17.d.3/0, where touch will be gained with the N.Z. Division.

The 1st Cheshires will be responsible for forming a defensive flank along BLEAK WALK to about SLUSH ALLEY, where touch with 16th R. War.R. will be gained.

The 1st Bedfords on left & 16th R. War.R. on right will follow in rear of 1st Norfolks side by side & will halt on the line of the Sunken Road through R.21.d. where they will be disposed in depth.

16th R. War.R. will push forward up GUN SUPPORT to meet 1st Cheshires.

Machine guns will be disposed to cover the right flank during the advance.

4. During the halt of the barrage on the general line of BARRACK TRENCH (see para. 2), 1st Cheshires will close well up to the barrage & 1st Norfolks will close up to 1st Cheshires.

As soon as the barrage lifts 1st Cheshires will occupy the trench system & 1st Norfolks will pass through.

5. 1st Cheshires & 1st Norfolks will advance on a wide front, working forward alongside trench lines on definite lines of advance.

ACKNOWLEDGE   P.T.O.

Issued at 9 pm.
29-9-1918.

Copies to:-
N° 1. 1st Norfolks.
2. 1st Bedfords. ✓
3. 1st Cheshires.
4. 16th R.War.R.
5. C Coy. M.G.C.
6. 62nd Infy. Bde.
7. 95th " "
8. 5th Divn. G.

J.G. Thail
Captain,
Brigade Major,
15th Infy. Brigade.

1st "Bedfordshire Reg'

October 1918.

CONFIDENTIAL.

Register No..............
Part No..............
Volume No..............

Vol 48

WAR DIARY

OF

2d Bedfordshire Regt

for the Month of

October 1918.

H.Q.
15TH INFANTRY BDE.
No. H. 1484
Dated 11.11.18

Brigadier-General,
Commanding 15th Infantry Brigade.

1/10/1918.

WAR DIARY
or
INTELLIGENCE SUMMARY.
(Erase heading not required.)

Army Form C. 2118.

Place	Date	Hour	Summary of Events and Information	Remarks and references to Appendices
	Oct. 1918. 1st.		Battalion withdrew to Huts at NEUVILLE. "A" Line Transport heavily shelled. Casualties :- One O.R. killed and One O.R. wounded. 3 Horses killed and 3 Horses wounded. Capt. F.W.Ballance, Lieuts. A.J.Tyson and B.L.Pavey, and 2/Lieuts. F.Flavell, and W.H.T. Cothill joined Battalion for duty.	
	2nd.		In Huts as above. Day devoted to bathing and cleaning up.	
	3rd.		As above. Training carried on.	
	4th.		Training carried on as above.	
	5th.		Training carried on as above.	
	6th.		Church Services for all denominations. Capt. W.J.Campion, Lieut. R.Caldwell-Cook and 2/Lieut. W.R.Hogg joined Battalion. Capt. J.C.A.Birch admitted to Field Ambulance sick.	
	7th.		Training carried on as above. 2/Lieuts. Hollingshead, R.B.Collins and C.O.Fowler joined Battalion for duty.	
	8th.		Training as above. Lieut. A.C.Holborow, and 2/Lieuts. B.L.Walker, D.J.Roberts, A.E.Davis and F.C.Foote joined Battalion.	
	9th.		Battalion marched to LA VACQUERIE.	App. I.
	10th.		Battalion marched to just South of ESNES.	App II.

Army Form C. 2118.

WAR DIARY
~~INTELLIGENCE~~ SUMMARY.
(Erase heading not required.)

Instructions regarding War Diaries and Intelligence Summaries are contained in F. S. Regs., Part II. and the Staff Manual respectively. Title pages will be prepared in manuscript.

Place	Date	Hour	Summary of Events and Information	Remarks and references to Appendices
	11th.		Battalion marched to LIGNY en CAMBRESIS, and billetted in houses.	App III.
	12th.		Battalion marched to CAUDRY. Town occupied by a large number of civilians. Troops billetted in houses.	App. IV.
	13th.		Church Services for all denominations.	
	14th.		Billetted as above. Training carried on. Concert in the evening. Lt. Col. C. E. G. Shearman, D.S.O., M.C. joined Battalion and assumed Command.	
	15th.)			
	16th.)			
	17th.)		Billetted as above, and training carried on.	
	18th.)			
	19th.		Ceremonial Parade. Corps Commander presents Medal Ribbons to those awarded decorations in August and September. Battalion (less Dumped Personnel) moved to BETHENCOURT. Dumped Personnel remained in CAUDRY.	App. V.
	20th.		Battalion moved at 04.30 hours to Quarry near River SELLE, afterwards crossing the river about 100 yards from the Quarry, and dug in by Railway Line. Situation normal.	
	21st.		In position as above.	

Army Form C. 2118.

WAR DIARY
or
INTELLIGENCE SUMMARY.
(Erase heading not required.)

Instructions regarding War Diaries and Intelligence Summaries are contained in F.S. Regs. Part II. and the Staff Manual respectively. Title pages will be prepared in manuscript.

Place	Date	Hour	Summary of Events and Information	Remarks and references to Appendices
	22nd.		Moved up from above position at night to assembly positions about E.22.c.7.8. to E.16.c.2.1. Enemy put down a barrage on the position. (Counter preparation)	
	23rd.		At 03.20 hours Bedfords and Cheshires went over the top to the attack, but were held up on the right by M.G. fire. Made good later on, capturing the village of BEAURAIN. Relieved during the day, and returned to billets in CAUDRY. Casualties – 2/Lieuts. W.H.T.Cothill and C.O.Fowler killed. Lt. Col. C.E.G.Shearman, D.S.O., M.C. Capt. F.W.Ballance, 2/Lieuts. H.Trasler, S.G.Fisher, J.Hollingshead, B.L.Walker, and the Rev. J.B.Mayall wounded. Lieut. B.L.Pavey, sick. 14 O.R. killed, 105 O.R. wounded and 5 O.R. missing.	App. VI. & VII.
	24th.		In billets as above, resting and cleaning up.	
	25th.		As above. Reorganisation of Companies.	
	26th.		As above. Battalion allotted baths. Other parades under Coy. arrangements.	
	27th.		As above. Church Services for all denominations.	
	28th.		As above. Battalion Training carried on.	
	29th.)			
	30th.)		As above Training as above.	
	31st.		As above. Training as above.	

Major.
Commanding 1st. Battalion The Bedfordshire Regiment.

SECRET.   (AM I)
                                                                    Copy No.
OPERATION   ORDER   No. 168.

                 1st. Battalion Bedfordshire Regiment.
Ref. Map Sheet 57.c. 1/20,000. (S.E.)   Oct. 9th. 1918.

1. The Battalion will move to-day to area North of GOUZEACOURT – MASNIERES
    Road in Squares R.16. R.17. and R.22.a.
2. ROUTE and TIME.   The Head of the Battalion will pass the cross roads
    at. P.29a.5.7. at 13.00 hours, and proceed via METZ Road to Brigade
    starting point at METZ Cross Roads, thence to GOUZEACOURT, and along
    main GOUZEACOURT – CAMBRAI Road, until met by guides of billeting party.
3. ORDER of MARCH.   H.Q., Drums. "A", "B", "C", and "D" Coy. Transport.
    Drums will fall back to Companies in turn at each halt.
    200 yards interval will be kept between Companies.
    Strict march discipline will be observed.
4. DRESS.   Full marching order. Leather Jerkins will be carried on the
    tops of packs.   Steel Helmets strapped on back.
5. Officers Valises will be ready for loading outside Coy. H.Q. at 11.00
    hours.   Orderly Room Boxes and Canteen Boxes will be ready at the same
    hour
6. Mess Boxes will be ready at 12.00 hours.
7. Lewis Guns will be loaded at Transport Lines at 10.30 hours. Sgt. Faulder
    will superintend loading.
    Lewis Gun Limbers will march in rear of their Companies.
8. Dinners at 11.45 hours.   Teas on arrival.
9. Marching out states will be handed to Adjutant before marching off.
    On arrival in new area, Companies and R.S.M. will report present or
    otherwise to Battalion Headquarters.

    ACKNOWLEDGE.

                                                    Capt. & A/Adjt.
                                             1st. Battalion Bedfordshire Regiment.

Copies to :-
    1. H.Q. 15th. Infy. Bde.
    2. Commanding Officer.
    3. O.C. "A" Coy.
    4. "   "B" "
    5. "   "C" "
    6. "   "D" "
    7. T.O.
    8. Q.M.
    9. R.S.M.
    10. File.
    11, 12, and 13. War Diary.

Oct 1918.

Oct 1918.

SECRET.

(W II)

Copy No.

OPERATION ORDER No. 169.

1st. Battalion The Bedfordshire Regiment.

Map Ref. Sheet 57.B. and 57.C.   Oct. 10th. 1918.

The Battalion will move to-day to Area in Square N.3. (57.B)
2. ROUTE. Lieut. B.L.Payex will meet Bde. Intelligence Officer to reconnoitre route at. M.16.a.8.9. at 09.00 hours
3. TIME. Head of Battalion will pass Battalion Headquarters at 10.35 hours, and will proceed via main CAMBRAI Road and pass Bde. Starting point at M.15.b.6.2. at 11.47 hours.
4. ORDER OF MARCH. H.Q., Drums, "B", "C", "D" and "A" Coy's. Drums will fall back one Coy. at each halt.
5. Billeting Party the same as yesterday will meet the Staff Captain at N.1.b.2.4. at 09.30 hours.
6. All surplus baggage and kit will be dumped, probably at LESDAIN. Location will be notified later.
7. Dinners on arrival xxx in new area.
8. Blankets, rolled in bundles of 10, will be dumped on the road, at the same place as drawn from yesterday, by 09.00 hours.

Capt. & A/Adjt.
1st. Battalion Bedfordshire Regiment.

SECRET.   Copy No
          OPERATION   ORDER   No. 170.

                1st. Battalion The Bedfordshire Regiment.
     Map Ref. 57.B. 1/40,000.   Oct. 11th. 1918.

1. The Battalion will move to-day to LIGNY en CAMBRESIS, and will probably
   move on to CAUDRY during the afternoon.
2. ROUTE and TIME.   Route via Cross Country tracks to be reconnoitred by
   Lt. J.C.Meade.   Battalion will move cross country at 08.35 hours and will
   pass Bde. Starting point at N.5.c.8.8. at 09.07 hours.
3. ORDER of MARCH.   H.Q., Drums, "C", "D" "A" and "B".
                Drums will fall back one Coy. at each halt.
4. On arrival, Battalion will concentrate about O.3.d.3.7. and will await
   orders.
5. Billeting party, same as detailed yesterday, will hold itself in readiness
   to meet the Staff Captain when the Battalion arrives at O.3.d.3.7.
6. Officers Valises, Mess Boxes etc., to be ready for loading at Q.M. Stores
   by 07.30 hours.
   Blankets, rolled in bundles of 10 to be at the Q.M. Stores by 07.00
   hours.
7. "B" Echelon and Dumped personnel will move with the Battalion.
8. Dinners will be eaten at O.3.d.3.7.

                                                    Capt. & A/Adjt.
                        1st. Battalion Bedfordshire Regiment.

SECRET.   OPERATION ORDER No. 171.   Copy No.

1st. Battalion The Bedfordshire Regiment.

Oct.-12th./18.

1. The Battalion will move to CAUDRY this afternoon, and will take over billets from 1st. Devonshire Regt.

2. ROUTE and TIME. Head of Battalion will pass Cross Roads at O.3.b.90.25. at 14.35 hours, and will be clear of the outskirts of LIGNY at I.34.d.2.5. by 15.00 Hours Troops will be kept off main roads as much as possible, Tracks beside the roads being made use of.

3. ORDER of MARCH. H.Q., Drums, "D", "A", "B" and "C" Coy's. Drums will fall back one Company at each halt.

4. 500 yards will be observed between Units, and 100 yards between Coy's. Battalion will be met outside CAUDRY and guided to billets by billeting party previously detailed.

5. Billeting certificates will be rendered to Orderly Room two hours after arrival. Blankets, Mess Boxes, Orderly Room Boxes, and Officers Kits as previously instructed.

Capt. & A/Adjt.

1st. Battalion Bedfordshire Regiment.

SECRET.   OPERATION   ORDER   No. 172.   Copy No.

1st. Battalion The Bedfordshire Regiment.

Oct. 19th. 1918.

1. **MOVE.** The Battalion will move to BETHENCOURT on night of 19th/20th. 1918.

2. **ROUTE and TIME.** Battalion will parade opposite Billets ready to march off at 21.40 hours, and the head of the column will cross the CAMBRAI - LE CATEAU Road at 22.00 hours.

3. **ORDER of MARCH.** Headquarters, "A", "D", "C", and "B" Coy's. Intervals of 200 yards between Companies and 100 yards between each group of 6 vehicles.

4. **BLANKETS.** Will be rolled in bundles of 10, clearly labelled and dumped for collection by Transport Officer at 15.00 hours. Officers Kits at about 16.00 hours, and Coy. Mess Boxes will be ready for collection at 20.00 hours.

5. **DRILL.** Full Marching Order.

6. **GUIDES.** Companies will be met before entering BETHENCOURT, by Coy. Guides.

7. **SURPLUS PERSONNEL.** will remain at CAUDRY with the exception of Drums, who will accompany the Battalion to BETHENCOURT, and will collect blankets and any other Dumped Kit, in the event of a sudden move. Drums will report to Rear Battn. H.Q., CAUDRY, in the event of a further move. All Transport will move with the Battalion, and will remain with Units until further orders.

On arrival at BETHENCOURT, 3 men of "C" Coy. will report immediately to 15th. T.M.Battery, to act as carriers. They will be rationed to 20th. inst. inclusive.

2/Lieut. S.W.P.Robinson, will report to 15th. Infy. Bde. H.Q. at 22.00 hours on the 19th. Oct. for synchronization of watches.

Capt. & A/Adjt.
1st. Battalion Bedfordshire Regiment.

Copies to :-
1. H.Q., 15th. Infy. Bde.
2. Commanding Officer.
3. O.C. "A" Coy.
4. "   "B" "
5. "   "C" "
6. "   "D" "
7. T.O.
8. Q.M.
9. R.S.M.
10. File.
11, 12 and 13. War Diary.

Oct 1918

Oct 1918

SECRET.   Copy No.

OPERATION ORDER No. 173.

1st. Battalion The Bedfordshire Regiment.

Map, Sheet 57.B. N.E., 1/20,000.   Oct. 22nd. 1918.

1. The advance will be resumed on the 23rd. Oct. 1918.
2. The 5th. Division will attack on the right of the IV Corps and the 42nd. Division on the left. The 21st. Division (V Corps) will attack on the right of the 5th. Division.
3. The 95th. Infantry Brigade will continue to hold the line. The 15th. Infantry Brigade will assemble in rear of the present front line and will pass through the 95th. Infantry Brigade, and capture the high ground East of BEAURAIN Village.
4. PLAN OF ATTACK. The 1st. Bedfordshire Regiment will attack on the right of the 15th. Infantry Brigade. The 1st. Cheshire Regiment on the left. The 1st. Norfolk Regiment will be in support, remaining in readiness about E.21.a. and c.
   The Battalion will attack on a two Company front as follows :-
       "A" Coy. on the right.) Up to the
       "B" " " left.) GREEN Line.
   Both Companies on a four platoon front. "C" and "D" Companies each on a three platoon front with one platoon in support of "A" and "B" Coy's. respectively.
   "C" and "D" Coy's. will pass through "A" and "B" Coy's. on the GREEN Line, and advance and capture the RED Line.
   "A" and "B" Coy's. will each detail two platoons to follow in close support of "C" and "D" Coy's. for mopping up as follows :-
       "A" Coy. up to and including line of SUNKEN Road from E.12.c.8.0. to E.12.c.0.6.
       "B" Coy. BEAURAIN Village south of Left Battalion boundary.
   Subsequent to mopping up these platoons will consolidate and hold a line running approximately 100 yards East of Road E.12.c.8.0. to E.11.b.7.3.
   Two Tanks will co-operate in the attack and have been allotted the task of assisting in mopping up of the SUNKEN Road E.16.a. to E.10.d. and Village of BEAURAIN.
   At a time to be notified later a Brigade of 37th. Division will pass through the 15th. Infantry Brigade on the RED Line and continue the pursuit.
5. BOUNDARIES. Right Battalion Boundary - E.22.d.0.5. to E.17.d.0.5. to E.12.c.8.0. to F.7.a.0.5.
       Left Battalion Boundary - E.16.c.0.0. to E.17.a.0.8. to E.11.c.7.6. to E.11.b.4.0. to E.11.b.6.3. to E.6.c.5.1.
       Inter Company Boundary - E.22.a.5.3. to E.16.d.7.5. to E.11.d.5.0. to E.12.c.0.6. to E.12.b.0.4.
6. ASSEMBLY. The Battalion will leave present positions at 21.00 hours on night of 22nd./23rd. Oct. 1918, and will assemble on the line E.22.c.8.8. to E.16.c.2.1. (Junction with 1st. Cheshires) Companies will move in the order A, B, C, D, and H.Q. and will form up as per diagram attached. Route from present positions to assembly will be notified later.
   Marking Officers of 1st. Bedfords and 1st. Cheshires with 8 markers and two guides per Battalion will meet the Brigade Major at Brigade Advanced Report Centre at E.21.b.6.2. at 21.00 hours 22nd. Oct. 1st. Bedfords will be clear of the Cross Roads at E.19.a.99.10. by 22.00 hours.
7. MACHINE GUNS. Subsequent to capture of RED Line, two Sections of "C" Coy. 5th. M.G.Battalion will take up positions approximately as follows :-
       1 Sect. - E.12.d.2.8.
       1 Sect. - E.12.c. central.
   These sections will move forward independent of the Battalion.
8. ARTILLERY. The attack will be carried out under a creeping barrage of Field Artillery. Details as to rate of advance will be issued later.
   A M.G. barrage is also being arranged which will be furnished by two Companies of 5th. M.G. Battalion.

9. **LIGHT T.M's.** 2 Guns will assemble in rear of the Battalion. These will move forward by bounds at a considerable distance in rear of the Battalion, and be carried by Pack animals. O!s.C. leading Companies will send back for one gun per Company if and when required.

10. **HEADQUARTERS.** Battalion Headquarters will be at approximately S.21.b. central. Advanced report Centre will move in rear of junction of "C" and "D" Companies, and will be established about d.17.b.1.6. as soon as all Companies pass this point. Upon capture of objectives, Coy. Headquarters will be established as follows :-

    "A" Coy. about S.17.b.3.0.
    "B" "   "   S.11.d.0.4.
    "C" "   "   S.12. central.
    "D" "   "   S.12.a.5.4.

11. **DRESS.** Battle order. 1 Rifle Grenade per man.
    1 Round V.P.A. per man.
    1 Days rations.
    1 Iron Ration.

12. **SIGNALS.** White Very Lights will be fired on the capture of each objective.

13. **SYNCHRONISATION.** An Officer from Battalion Headquarters will visit Companies for purpose of synchronizing watches during the early hours of the 23rd. inst.

14. **ZERO HOUR.** Zero hour will be notified later.

                                        Capt. & A/Adjt.
                                        1st. Battalion Bedfordshire Regiment.

1st. Battalion The Bedfordshire Regiment.

Addendum to Operation Order No. 173, dated 22/10/18.

1. Ref. para. 1. 7th. Leicesters will attack on night of this Battalion. 8th. Leicesters will pass through them on RED Line.
2. Ref. para. 4. (Plan of Attack) The two platoons of "A" Coy. detailed for mopping up behind "C" Coy. will consolidate a line running approximately E.12.c.3.8. to E.18.a.3.5.
   The support platoon of "C" Coy. will consolidate a line running E.12.d.2.4. to E.12.d.2.8.
   Support platoons of "C" and "D" Coy's. will move in rear of the right leading platoon of these Companies and will be prepared to defend the right flank of their Companies should the situation so demand.
   The 111th. Brigade (37th. Divn) are due to pass through 15th. Infy. Bde. on RED Line at 08.40 hours.
3. Ref. para. 8. (Artillery) The barrage will dwell for 6 minutes on the initial line (E.22.b.2.2. to E.16.a.0.6.) and then move forward at the rate of 100 yards in six minutes.
   A dwell of 12 minutes will be made on the GREEN Line.
4. Ref. para. 9. (Light T.M's.) Light T.M's. will not move forward from about E.20. central till dawn.
5. Four Tanks will assist in mopping up BEAURAIN.
6. Contact Planes will call for flares at 07.00 hours.
7. Zero hour will be 03.20 hours on 23rd. Oct. 1918.
8. Compass Bearing for all Companies is 48 degrees. (True).

Captain & A/Adjt.
1st. Battalion Bedfordshire Regiment.

Oct. 1918

Oct 1918.

5th DIVISION SUMMARY OF INFORMATION.
25th October 1918.

OPERATIONS.
Third Army.

During the night 23rd/24th October BEAUDIGNIES was captured and a bridgehead formed East of it. The attack was resumed on the 24th, in conjunction with the Armies on each flank. Considerable opposition was again experienced on the right, but in spite of it POIX DU NORD, WAGONVILLE, ENGLEFONTAINE, and CHISSIGNIES were captured. East of BEAUDIGNIES resistance stiffened but to the North RUESNES was taken.

From G.H.Q. timed 09.45 hrs. today :-
S. of the OISE the FRENCH attacked on front CHEVRIES - LUCY and took 350 prisoners. S. of DEYNZE FRENCH have reached COURTRAI - DEYNZE Road E. of OLSEN.
In FLANDERS the FRENCH have taken WAEREGHEM with 200 prisoners.

INTELLIGENCE.

AERIAL. to 16 hrs. 24th. - Nearly 2 tons of bombs were dropped of which ½ ton was dropped on LE QUESNOY Station on the evening of the 23rd, and nearly 1½ tons on various ground targets during the 24th. 190 rounds were fired.

ENEMY DEFENCES. Photographs taken on 23rd. show no defences dug in the following squares :- R.19.c. and d., 11.c. & d., 15.b. and d. 16, 17, 21.b. 22.a. and b. 23.a.

DISTRIBUTION OF ENEMY'S FORCES.

111th Div.
76th I.R. (1st Bn.) SALESCHES. Oct 24th.
A prisoner of the 76th I.R. was found hiding a SALESCHES. He stated that his divisional train was at JOLIMETZ. It is possible that the 76th I.R. is on this front but this prisoner was probably a straggler and the presence of the Regt. is doubtful.

4th Division.
140th I.R. (all Bns) S. of CHISSIGNIES. Oct.24th - Prisoner.
14th I.R. (1st & 3rd Bns.) near RUESNES. " "

185th Division.
28th R.I.R. near CHISSIGNIES. October 24th. Prisoner.
65th I.R. do. do.

58th Division.
106 I.R. (3rd Bn.) S.W. of CHISSIGNIES. Oct. 24th. Prisoner.

25th Division.
45th Bearer Coy. - VENDEGIES area. Oct. 23rd. Prisoner.
I Pnr. Bn.3rd Coy. do. do.

Miscellaneous.
The 25th and 1st Gd. Res. Divn. are considered to have been withdrawn also elements of the 9th Res. Divn.

Disbanding of the 25th Res. Division.

Later prisoners of the 168th I.R. taken yesterday afternoon state that the other two Regts. of the 25th Res. Divn., the 83rd and 118th R.I.Rs. were broken up last week.

2.

INTENTIONS.

On this front, the only orders prisoners had received were to hold on, and they knew nothing of any retirement.

The Army on our left reports that the Canal line near ST AMAND is to be held for a few days only, and then a withdrawal will take place to a line near MONS.

Civilians report that the banks of the ESCAUT near VALENCIENNES are mined for flooding the country. Civilians were evacuated from W. of this line to NIVELLES owing to the proposed inundations, and also to work on defences near NAMUR and LIEGE. The defences at CONDE and MAULDE are confirmed.

A Platoon Commander of the 87th R.I.R., 21st Res. Divn. states that the enemy is endeavouring to hold on until the system RETHEL - MAUBEUGE - MONS is completed. Pioneers of the 21st Res. Divn., after our attack on the line LE CATEAU - ST QUENTIN were sent to the vicinity of MAUBEUGE to help to complete this system.

SUMMARY.

The presence of one Regt. of the 58th Divn. is significant, considering that the other two Regts. are in line near VALENCIENNES, in that it shows that the enemy has few reserves available and is forced to move a Regt. from one Army Sector to that of another.

The 4th Divn. which was in Army Reserve, appears to have been put in peacemeal to reinforce weak sectors.

The enemy's forces seem to be considerably disorganised.

The only orders which appear to have been issued, are to hold on. Prisoners state that a defensive line is in course of construction about RETHEL - MAUBEUGE - MONS, but that it is not yet completed, and that our advance is consequently to be delayed as long as possible.

EXTRACTS FROM CAPTURED DOCUMENT.

(a) Div. Order of 25th Divn. dated 15/10/18. "The D.C. is expecting a renewal of the attack by the enemy from NEUVILLY North through SOLESMES. The task of the Division is to hold the railway as the main line of resistance and deny to the enemy crossings of the River SELLE.

(b) Garrison of South Tank Fort on Road in E.8.a.3/0.:-

2 L.T.M's. with 100 rounds each.
1 M.T.M.
1 Field Gun. 180 rounds.
2 Heavy M.G. 4,000 rounds armour piercing.

Personnel - 1 Officer, 3 Sgt. Majors, 7 N.C.O's. 33 O.R.
The Fort was connected by telephone with H.Q."

PRISONERS.

18.00 hrs. 23rd to 18.00 hrs. 24th :-

	Officers.	O.R.
Unwounded.	82.	2,000
Wounded.	7.	234
	89	2,234.
Since Oct.1st.	404	14,811.
Since Aug.21st.	1,513	55,988.

The total number of Guns captured by the Army from the 21st Aug. to the 19th October is 486.

25th October 1918.

INTELLIGENCE.
5th Division.

A. Coy
B. WC
C.
D.

I.O.

Please pass quickly [signature] Adjutant,
BEDFORDSHIRE REGT.

REPORT ON PRISONERS CAPTURED DURING RECENT OPERATIONS.

In our attack on October 20th, 3 Officers and 338 O.Rs. were captured. The enemy Divisions holding the Sector opposite us were the 25th and 1st Guard Reserve divisions. The 25th Division, which was chiefly involved in the attack, was classed as a "counter-attack division" and had been out of the line for 6 weeks. It was strong and fresh and had been put in the line with definite orders to hold the RAILWAY EMBANKMENT at all costs. They had been told that this position was of vital importance and that support and reserve troops were to move forward and counter-attack in the event of the BRITISH gaining a footing there. All 3 Regiments of this Division were in the line, each with one battalion forward, one in support and one in reserve. Our attack in the early morning accounted for the forward battalions of each Regt., the survivors of which retired to the positions of the support battalions. When our attack was continued in the afternoon the support battalions were similarly disposed and there remained only the reserve battalions of each Regiment which hurriedly put up a defensive position West of BEAURAIN. Meanwhile a battalion of the 4th Division was hurriedly pushed forward in the evening of the 20th instant, and took up a position in the outskirts of BEAURAIN, with orders to hold the Village.

Meanwhile the 1st Guard Reserve Division, which had come into the line in a very weak state, had suffered heavily and was unable to hold its sector. Consequently the 30th Division, which was resting after heavy engagements on this front, was brought forward and put in the line between the 25th and the 1st Guard Res. Divns. At the same time the enemy's artillery was reinforced, so that the enemy was prepared to offer strong resistance to us when we continued our attack on the morning of October 23rd. His orders were again to the effect that no retirement was to take place.

In our attack on October 23rd we captured 3 Officers and 88 O.R's., among the Officers was a battalion commander and his adjutant.

It has already been stated that the enemy's intentions were to hold his positions at all costs. In no case did it appear that we outnumbered the enemy, and prisoners themselves attributed our successes first to the superior morale of our troops and secondly to our preponderance of artillery. Prisoners of the Field Artillery of the 25th Division declared that a comparison between BRITISH and GERMAN artillery would be absurd and that they had never seen such a concentration of Heavy Arty. as that through which they had passed on their way to the Cage. Infantrymen stated that GERMAN artillery continually fires short and that Gunners have told them that complaints are useless as the guns are worn out and unreliable, they added that the heavy counter-preparation which the enemy put down on our front on the night October 22nd/23rd inflicted severe casualties on their own troops. High tributes were paid to the intensity and accuracy of our artillery fire and to the demoralising effect of the concentrations, to which we subjected the enemy's positions from time to time. Several prisoners testified to the effect of our Machine Guns and to the speed with which they took up

/advanced

2.

advanced positions and engaged fresh targets. One prisoner, the survivor of M.G. team, stated that his gun engaged a BRITISH M.G. team which they saw coming into action without success, whilst the BRITISH Gun got into action and knocked out the gun and team with the exception of himself. The enemy's horses are in a very bad condition, artillery prisoners expressed astonishment that our horses had stood the advance so well.

The morale of the prisoners generally was very low. Many had been told that an armistice was assured within a fortnight, if they would hold out so long; and in several cases they asked on arrival at the Cage if it were true that the Entente Powers were going to accept the KAISER'S peace offer. Leave had recently been stopped till October 28th and the current rumour was that this step had been taken to facilitate the evacuation of occupied territory. It appears that the enemy is doing his utmost to raise the dejected spirit of his troops by the promise of an early peace and that the more intelligent are beginning to doubt whether there is much foundation for these promises. A Battalion Commander, when invited to express his opinion on the final issue, said that he feared GERMANY would retain nothing that she had won but her fame. Other Officers affirmed that GERMANY'S only Reserves now are exhausted troops who are constantly being disturbed from a much-needed rest and sent back to the line. Men of the 1st Guard Res. Division related with bitterness that, as a punishment for retiring at CAMBRAI, they had been put back in the line in this Sector, their Divl. Commander having assured them that they would stay there till the whole Division could be fed from one Cooker.

In conclusion, it can be confidently stated that whereas prisoners taken by us a month ago were of opinion that final victory for GERMANY was impossible, those taken within the last few days regarded her defeat as certain.

25th October 1918.

INTELLIGENCE.
5th Division.

Volume No. _____

BRITISH SALONIKA FORCE

WAR DIARY.

Anti-Aircraft Sections.

Vol. No.	Unit	PERIOD From	To
20.	24th Anti-Aircraft Section	1.7.17	31.7.17
21.	39nd do.	–	–
10.	3rd do.		
4.	74th do.	1.5.17	31.5.17
6.	do.	1.7.17	31.7.17
5.	90th do.	–	–
6.	91st do.	–	–
5.	94th do.	–	–
4.	97th do.	–	–
4.	98th do.	1.7.17	31.7.17
1.	99th do.	16.7.17	31.7.17

A.P. & S.D., Alex./No. 752/8:5:17/3000 (5004IG/53) W.M. & Co.

1st Bedfordshire Regt

November 1918

WAR DIARY

OF

1st Bedfordshire Regt.

for the month of

November 1918.

Commanding 15th Infantry Brigade.

Army Form C. 2118.

WAR DIARY
or
INTELLIGENCE SUMMARY.
(Erase heading not required.)

Instructions regarding War Diaries and Intelligence Summaries are contained in F. S. Regs., Part II. and the Staff Manual respectively. Title pages will be prepared in manuscript.

Place	Date	Hour	Summary of Events and Information	Remarks and references to Appendices
	1918.			
	Nov. 1st.		Battalion billetted at CAUDRY.	
	" 2nd.		Battalion billetted at CAUDRY.	
	" 3rd.		Billetted as above. Battalion moved to NEUVILLE, via BETHENCOURT, BRIASTRE, SOLESMES and BEAURAIN. Dumped Personnel and "B" Echelon remained at BEAURAIN.	App. I.
	" 4th.		Battalion moved from NEUVILLE between 15.00 and 16.00 hours and marched to LOUVIGNES.	
	" 5th.		Battalion moved from LOUVIGNES at 02.00 hours and marched to JOLIMETZ. Passed through the 1st. Battalion Norfolk Regt. at 06.00 hours, and captured BLACK LINE without opposition. Advanced towards YELLOW LINE, considerable Machine Gun fire. Casualties - 7 O.R's. Battalion attacked at 15.15 hours, and gained objectives. Battalion Headquarters at LA CABINE.	
	" 6th.		Battalion advanced to LA PORQUERIE. Shelled out of the village in the morning and again at dusk. Casualties - 13 O.R's. During the above operations, the Battalion captured a 6" Naval Gun.	
	" 7th.		Battalion billetted in village of LA POUQUERIE. No enemy shelling.	
	" 8th.		As above.	
	" 9th.		As above.	
	" 10th.		Battalion marched to JOLIMETZ and billetted.	App. II.

WAR DIARY
or
INTELLIGENCE SUMMARY.
(Erase heading not required.)

Army Form C. 2118.

Instructions regarding War Diaries and Intelligence Summaries are contained in F. S. Regs., Part II, and the Staff Manual respectively. Title pages will be prepared in manuscript.

Place	Date	Hour	Summary of Events and Information	Remarks and references to Appendices
	Nov.11th.		ARMISTICE DECLARED. Everything quiet. Battalion marched to LOUVIGNES and billetted.	
	" 12th.		Battalion billetted as above.	
	" 13th.		Battalion marched to RAMPONEAU via LE QUESNOY, and billetted.	App. III.
	" 14th.		Battalion inspected by Brigadier General Commanding.	
	" 15th.		Battalion billetted in RAMPONEAU. Battalion smartening up in readiness for proposed move to GERMANY.	
	" 16th.)			
	" 17th.)		Billetted as above.	
	" 18th.)			
	" 19th.		As above. Lt. Col. C.E.G.Shearman, D.S.O., M.C. rejoined from Casualty Clearing Station.	
	" 20th.		Battalion moved to Billets in LE QUESNOY.	
	" 21st.		As above. Capt. J.C.A.Birch rejoined from Sick leave. Lieut. J.C.Meade and 2/Lieut. K.W.P. Harvey from Field Ambulance.	
	" 22nd.		Billetted as above. Battalion working on Demobilization Scheme, i.e., Educational, Recreational and ordinary Training.	

Army Form C. 2118.

WAR DIARY
or
INTELLIGENCE SUMMARY.
(Erase heading not required.)

Instructions regarding War Diaries and Intelligence Summaries are contained in F. S. Regs., Part II. and the Staff Manual respectively. Title pages will be prepared in manuscript.

Place	Date	Hour	Summary of Events and Information	Remarks and references to Appendices
	Nov. 23rd.			
	" 24th.		Billetted as above. Training as above. Capt. H.W.Wright, Lieuts. J.Kelk, A.Young, M.E.A.	
	" 25th.			
	" 26th.			
	" 27th.		Parr and R.Hall, and 2/Lieuts. J.C.M.Taylor and E.C.Herberg joined for duty.	
	" 28th.			
	" 29th.		Billetted as above. Brigade Route March.	
	" 30th.		Billetted as above. Training carried on.	

[signature] Lt. Colonel.
Commanding 1st. Battalion,
The Bedfordshire Regiment.

SECRET.   Copy No.

OPERATION   ORDER   No. 174.

1st. Battalion The Bedfordshire Regiment.
                                        Nov. 3rd. 1918.

1. The Battalion will move to BEAURAIN to-day Nov. 3rd. 1918.
2. ROUTE – Via BETHENCOURT – VIESLY – BRIASTRE – MAROU – BEAURAIN.
3. Time. Battalion will be formed up in Column of route, in Square,
   (I.24.a.9.8.) clear of traffic, ready to move at 16.45 hours.
4. Order of March.   H.Q., "A", "B", "C" and "D" Coy's.
   Intervals of 500 yards between Units and 100 yards between Companies
   and sections of Transport will be maintained.
5. Officers Kits and Orderly Room Boxes will be ready for collection by
   Transport Officer at 14.30 hours. Mess Boxes as previously arranged.
6. Damage Certificates will be rendered to Orderly Room by 16.00 hours.
   In cases of occupied billets, from owners, and unoccupied billets, from
   Town Major.
7. Guides from Billeting party will meet Battalion at BEAURAIN Church.
8. Lewis Gun Limbers and Cookers will move immediately behind their
   respective Coy's.
9. Teas will be at 15.15 hours. Hot food will be served on arrival.

                                    Capt. & A/Adjt.
                            1st. Battalion Bedfordshire Regiment.

SECRET.

OPERATION ORDER No. 176.

1st. Battalion The Bedfordshire Regiment.

Nov. 3th. 1918.

1. The Battalion will march to RAMPONSAU (M.20.a.) to-day Nov. 13th. 1918.
2. ROUTE. Via Cross Roads at M.26.c. - Cross Roads at M.21.c. - Cross Roads at M.19.c. Bn. will pass Cross Roads at S.1.d.4.6. at 14.30 hours. Interval of 50 yards will be observed between Companies.
3. ORDER of MARCH. H.Q., "A", "B", "C" and "D" Coy's.
   Drums will march with each Coy. in turn.
4. Officers Kits will be sent to Quartermaster's Stores at once.

Capt. & A/Adjt.
1st. Battalion The Bedfordshire Regiment.

Secret.   Copy No.

O P E R A T I O N   O R D E R   No. 175.   APP II

1st. Battalion The Bedfordshire Regiment.
Map Ref. Sheet 5 . S.W. 1/20,000.   Nov. 10th, 1918.

1. The Battalion will move at once to JOLIMETZ, via LA GRANDE CARRIERE.
2. TIME.   Head of Battalion will pass EMBU FARM ("D" Coy's. H. .) at U.8.b at 13.45 hours.
3. ORDER OF MARCH.   Headquarters, "D", "A", "B", and "C" Coy's. and Transport.   Interval of 100 yards will be observed between Companies.
4. On arrival, Battalion will be met by guides outside village.

                                              Capt. & A/Adjt.
                             1st. Battalion The Bedfordshire Regiment.

Volume No. _____

BRITISH SALONIKA FORCE

WAR DIARY.

Anti-Aircraft Sections.

Vol. No.		Unit	PERIOD From	To
21.	24th	Anti-Aircraft Section	1.8.17	31.8.17
22.	32nd	do.	—	—
11.	43rd	do.	—	—
7.	74th	do.	—	—
6.	90th	do.	—	—
7.	91st	do.	—	—
6.	94th	do.	—	—
5.	97th	do.	—	—
5.	98th	do.	—	—
2.	99th	do.	—	—

1st Bedfordshire Regt

December 1918

Volume No. _____

BRITISH SALONIKA FORCE

WAR DIARY.

		PERIOD	
Vol. No.	Unit	From	To
15.	Bute Battery, R.G.A. (4th Highland Mountain Bde).	1. 5. 18.	31. 5. 18.

Register No..............
Part No..............
Volume No.............

WAR DIARY

of

1st Bedfordshire Regt

For the Month of

DECEMBER, 1918.

W.L.Osborn
Brigadier-General,
Commanding 15th Infantry Brigade.

CONFIDENTIAL.

Army Form C. 2118.

WAR DIARY
INTELLIGENCE SUMMARY.
(Erase heading not required.)

Place	Date	Hour	Summary of Events and Information	Remarks and references to Appendices
	1918			
	Dec. 1st.		Battalion billeted in LE QUESNOY. Training carried on as usual. His Majesty the KING passed through the Town in the morning.	
	" 2nd.		As above. His Majesty again passed through the Town.	
	" 3rd.		As above. Ceremonial Parade for visit to the Town of His Majesty the KING.	
	" 4th.		As above. His Majesty continued his inspection of the Town.	
	" 5th.)			
	" 6th.)			
	" 7th.)			
	" 8th.)		As above. Training carried on as usual.	
	" 9th.)			
	" 10th.)			
	" 11th.)			
	" 12th.)			
	" 13th.		Battalion marched to BELLIGNIES and Billeted. Battalion Headquarters in Chateau of Princess Leopold.	A/A I
	" 14th.		Battalion marched to NEUF-MESNIL and billetted.	

Army Form C. 2118.

WAR DIARY
INTELLIGENCE SUMMARY.
(Erase heading not required.)

Place	Date	Hour	Summary of Events and Information	Remarks and references to Appendices
	Dec. 15th.		Battalion marched to ROUBAIX and Billetted.	
	" 16th.		Battalion marched to CROIX le ROUVEROY and billetted.	
	" 17th.		Billetted as above. Battalion resting for 24 hours.	
	" 18th.		Battalion resumed march to HAINE St. PIERRE and billetted.	
	" 19th.		Battalion marched to MANAGE and billetted.	
	" 20th.		Battalion marched to NIEVELLES and Billetted. Regimental Colours joined the Battalion from England.	
	" 21st.		Battalion marched to SOMBREFFE and billetted.	
	" 22nd.		Battalion marched to GEMBLOUX and billetted. (Final Destination) Billets very good.	
	" 23rd.		Billetted as above.	
	" 24th.			
	" 25th.		Christmas Day. Church Services for all denominations.	
	" 26th.		Boxing Day. Holiday.	
	" 27th.			
	" 28th.		Billetted as above. School and Training carried on.	
	" 29th.			

WAR DIARY
INTELLIGENCE SUMMARY.
(Erase heading not required.)

Army Form C. 2118.

Place	Date	Hour	Summary of Events and Information	Remarks and references to Appendices
	Dec. 30th.		Billetted as above. School and Training carried on.	
	" 31st.			

Kilrick Capt. for Lt. Colonel.

Commanding 1st. Battalion The Bedfordshire Regiment.

SECRET.   No.
           O P E R A T I O N   O R D E R   177.

                     1st. Battalion The Bedfordshire Regiment.
                                                          Dec. 12th. 1918.

1. MOVE.   The 15th. Infantry Brigade will commence march to GEMBLOUX
            to-morrow the 13th. inst. as per Brigade March Table attached.
2. TIME.   The Battalion will parade in the Rue JUHEL ready to move off at
            08.53 hours.
                   Order of March - Headquarters, Drums, "A", "B", "C" and "D" Coy's.
                                    and Transport.
                Interval between Companies - 10 yards.
                Interval between Battalions - 30 yards.
3. HALTS.   No halts except the 10 minutes halt before each clock hour will
            be permitted. The Commanding Officer will sound one long whistle one
            minute before each clock hour, on which Coy. Commanders will order
            men to dress and fall in. At the clock hour, Commanding Officer will
            sound two whistles, whereupon Coy. Commanders will give order "Quick
            March."
4. DRESS.   Full Marching order. Leather Jerkins rolled on top of pack,
            Box Respirators on top of pack. Mess Tins inside pack. Steel Helmets
            in straps on back of packs.
5. BILLETING PARTY.   The following Billeting party will report to Orderly
            Room to-morrow at 07.00 hours.
                   2/Lieut. E.W.P. Robinson.
                   4 C.Q.M. Sgts.
                   1 N.C.O. for Headquarters.
                   1 N.C.O. for Tpt. and Q.M. Stores.
6. OFFICERS KITS, Orderly Room Boxes etc., will be ready for collection by
            07.30 hours. Mess Boxes at 08.00 hours.
            BLANKETS will be rolled in bundles of 10, labelled and taken to Q.M.
            Stores by 07.30 hours.
7. REVEILLE will be at 06.30 hours. Breakfasts at 07.00 hours.
8. SYNCHRONISATION. The Signalling Sergt. will ensure that all Officers
            receive the correct time at 07.00 hours to-morrow.

                                        R.N.C. Riddell   Captain & Adjt.
                                        1st. Battalion Bedfordshire Regiment.

Dec. 1918

Dec 1918

CONFIDENTIAL.

Jan–Apl 1919

No. 2572
Date 21/2/19
H.Q., 15TH INFANTRY BDE.

WAR DIARY

OF

1st Bedfordshire Regt

for the month of

January 1919.

Commanding 15th Infantry Brigade

1 & 2/1 1919.

Army Form C. 2118.

WAR DIARY
or
INTELLIGENCE SUMMARY

(Erase heading not required.)

Instructions regarding War Diaries and Intelligence Summaries are contained in F. S. Regs., Part II. and the Staff Manual respectively. Title Pages will be prepared in manuscript.

Place	Date	Hour	Summary of Events and Information	Remarks and references to Appendices
GEMBLOUX.	1/1/19. To 9/1/19.		In billets in Gembloux. Education and Training carried on. Sports held every afternoon weather permitting.	
	10/1/19.		As above. Photographs of Officers, Sergeants, and Corporals taken.	
	11/1/19. To 16/1/19.		In billets as above. Training etc as above.	
	17/1/19. To 23/1/19.		In billets as above. Training and Sports as above.	
	24/1/19.		As above. Divisional General visited Battalion.	
	25/1/19.		As above. Rehearsal for the Trooping of the Colours at Louze.	
	26/1/19.		As above. Rehearsal for the Trooping of the Colours at Gembloux.	
	27/1/19.		As above.	
	28/1/19.		Ceremonial Parade for Trooping the Regimental Colours in Place St. Aubyn, Namur, together with the 2nd. Battalion Kings Own Scottish Borderers. This ceremony was performed in commemoration of the taking of the town and citadel of Namur in 1695, in which this Battalion and the 2nd. Battalion Kings Own Scottish Borderers took part. Reviewing Officer :- Lt.General, Sir G.M.Harper K.C.B., D.S.O. Commanding 4th Corps.	

Officer Commanding the Colour Guard :- Captain J.C.A.Birch.
Lieutenant of the escort :- Lt. A. Young.
2/Lt. for the Colour :- 2/Lt. R. Forbes.

2449 Wt. W14957/M90 750,000 1/16 J.R.T.& A. Forms/C2118/12. N.C.O. for the COLOUR. 10339. C.S.M. F.Meade.

Army Form C. 2118.

WAR DIARY
or
INTELLIGENCE SUMMARY
(Erase heading not required.)

Place	Date	Hour	Summary of Events and Information	Remarks and references to Appendices
GEMBLOUX.	29/1/19.		Photographs of Battalion taken and also of the Colour Guard and Escort.	
	30/1/19.		Training and Sports carried on as usual.	
	31/1/19.		As above.	

Signed: Lt. Colonel.
Commanding 1st Battalion The Bedfordshire Regiment.

CONFIDENTIAL.

Register........
Part No:........
Volume No:...... Vol 52

WAR DIARY

OF

1st Bedfordshire Regt
─────────────────
for the month of
February   1919.
─────────────────

R.O.Brown Briv Genl
─────────────────
15th Infantry Brigade
Commanding

1/57/19B.

Army Form C. 2118.

WAR DIARY
or
INTELLIGENCE SUMMARY

(Erase heading not required.)

Instructions regarding War Diaries and Intelligence Summaries are contained in F. S. Regs., Part II. and the Staff Manual respectively. Title Pages will be prepared in manuscript.

Place	Date	Hour	Summary of Events and Information	Remarks and references to Appendices
GEMBLOUX.	1st 2nd		In billets in Gembloux. Usual training and in morning and games in afternoon. "	
	3rd		100 men visited Waterloo by lorries with Commanding Officer. Remainder training as above.	
	4th 5th 6th 7th 8th		Training and games as above.	
	9th		Church Services for all Denominations.	
	10th		Training and games carried on. Cross Country Race, Battalion Team 20 finished out of 25 thereby winning race medals for runners and Cup for Battalion.	
	11th		Training as above.	
	12th 13th 14th 15th		As above.	
	16th		Church Service for all Denominations.	
	17th 18th 19th 20th 21st 22nd		As above. Demobilization of Battalion practically finished.	

2449 Wt. W14957/Mg0 750,000 1/16 J.B.C. & A. Forms/C.2118/12.

Army Form C. 2118.

WAR DIARY
or
INTELLIGENCE SUMMARY

(Erase heading not required.)

Instructions regarding War Diaries and Intelligence Summaries are contained in F. S. Regs., Part II and the Staff Manual respectively. Title Pages will be prepared in manuscript.

Place	Date	Hour	Summary of Events and Information	Remarks and references to Appendices
	23rd		Church Service for all Denominations.	
	24th		Training and Sports as above. The Brigadier General presented Cup to Battalion Cross Country Team.	
	25th		As above.	
	26th		Draft of 2 Officers and 143 O.R.s (for Rhine) proceeded to Calais to join 11th Suffolk Regt, 61st Division.	
	27th		As above.	
	28th		As above. Mobilization stores despatched to Charleroi dump.	

[signature] Lt. Colonel,

Commanding 1st Battalion The Bedfordshire Regiment.

Army Form C. 2118.

WAR DIARY
or
INTELLIGENCE SUMMARY

(Erase heading not required.)

Nov 53

56°

Place	Date	Hour	Summary of Events and Information	Remarks and references to Appendices
GEMBLOUX.	1		Battalion billetted in Gembloux.	
	2		Battalion Band arrived from England.	
	3			
	4			
	5		Billetted as above	
	6			
	7		As above. General and Lady Haking Inspected Company Banners of the Division at the Hotel de Ville Gembloux.	
	8		Billetted as above.	
	9		Church Service for all Denominations.	
	10			
	11		As above.	
	12		As above. Divisional Dinner for Officers at Brussels.	
	13			
	14		Billetted as above.	
	15			
	16		As above. Church Service for all Denominations.	
	17			
	18			
	19		Billetted as above	
	20			
	21			
	22			
	23		As above. Church Service for all Denominations	

Instructions regarding War Diaries and Intelligence Summaries are contained in F. S. Regs., Part II. and the Staff Manual respectively. Title Pages will be prepared in manuscript.

2449 Wt. W14957/M90 750,000 1/16 J.B.C. & A. Forms/C.2118/12.

WAR DIARY or INTELLIGENCE SUMMARY

(Erase heading not required.)

Army Form C. 2118.

Place	Date	Hour	Summary of Events and Information	Remarks and references to Appendices
	24		As above.	
	25			
	26			
	27		As above.	
	28		As above. Lt. Colonel C.E.G. Shearman D.S.O.,M.C. detailed to join 53rd Battalion The Bedfordshire Regiment on expiration of leave.	
	29		As above. Church Service for all Denominations. Capt. G. McM.Betty M.C. Capt. W. Hobbs M.C. Capt. W.J. Campion M.C. Capt. A.J. Fyson	
	30		Lieut. R. Hall 2/Lt. F. Whateley Knight, proceeded to join 52nd Battalion The Bedfordshire Regiment.	
	31			

W. C. Leask. Major.

Commanding 1st Battalion The Bedfordshire Regiment.

Army Form C. 2118.

WAR DIARY
or
INTELLIGENCE SUMMARY
(Erase heading not required.)

Instructions regarding War Diaries and Intelligence Summaries are contained in F.S. Regs., Part II. and the Staff Manual respectively. Title Pages will be prepared in manuscript.

Place	Date	Hour	Summary of Events and Information	Remarks and references to Appendices
GEMBLOUX	APRIL		Battalion Billetted in GEMBLOUX	
	1			
	2			
	3			
	4			
	5			
	6		As above, Battalion preparing for move to GILLY, first stage in journey to England	App. 1
	7		Battalion moved to GILLY and billetted. See B.O.178	
	8		As above.	
	9		As above, Captain W.C.Segrle proceeded to join the 52nd Battalion The Bedfordshire Regiment.	
	10		As above.	
	11		As above, 2/Lieuts. E.C.Howlett and D.Lydle proceeded to England. 2/Lieuts. L.G.Cale and B.W.P.Robinson to 5th Divisional Details Battalion	
	12		As above	
	13			
	14			
	15			
	16		As above, Received orders for entrainment on 17th.	
	17		Battalion marched to HAUTEVILLE Station, CHARLEROI and entrained, train moved off at 19.00 hours. See O.O.179	App. 2
	18		In Camp as above.	
	19		As above	
	20		Embarked for England.	
ANTWERP	20/4/19		Commanding 1st Battalion The Bedfordshire Regiment	Lieut.,

APP 2

OPERATION ORDERS NO. 179
===

1st Battalion The Bedfordshire Regiment

16th April 1919

1. **MOVE** Battalion will entrain for ANTWERP tomorrow. Battalion will Parade in front of Q.M.Stores at 12.00 hours.
   Dress Marching Order less packs, Water-bottles to be filled.

2. **REVEILLE** Reveille will be at 06.30 hours.

3. **MEALS** Breakfast will be at 07.30 hours, dinners at 11.00 hours.

4. **KITS** Officers' kits, blankets, in bundles of ten, packs etc. to be at Q.M.Stores by 11.00 hours.

5. **COLOUR PARTY** The following W.O. & N.C.O.s will form the Colour Party for the journey:-
   C.S.M. J.T.Trundley D.C.M.
   Sgt. T.Bryan D.C.M.
   " A.Driver

LOADING PARTY C.S.Alley and 6 O.R.s from the Band will proceed to HAUTEVILLE Station level crossing at 08.00 hours and will meet lorry there at 08.30 hours. They will proceed with lorry to the Barracks CHARLEROI and load Band boxes etc.

A.W.Rhino Lieut., & A/Adjutant,
1st BEDFORDSHIRE REGT.

OPERATION ORDERS NO. 178

1st Battalion The Bedfordshire Regiment.

6th. April 1919

1 MOVE
The Battalion will move to GILLY tomorrow, parade at Orderly Room at 09.25 hours-"- Dress Marching Order less packs. Water bottles to be filled, Water proof sheets to be carried

2 KITS
Officers kits, blankets, packs, and Orderly Room boxes to be taken to Q.M. Stores by 08-30 hours
Band boxes etc. will be ready for loading at "A" Chateau by 09-00 hours.

3 REVEILLE
Reveille will be at XXXXXXX 06-30 hours

4 Breakfasts
Breakfast will be at 7-30 hours

5 Advance Party
Corpl. Diemer and 1 O.R. will go with first lorry leaving Q.M. Stores at XXXXXX 09-00 hours

6 DINNERS
Dinner will be on arrival in billets. All ranks are warned to carry the unexpired portion of the days rations with them as no haversack ration will be issued.

7 MARCHING STATE
Marching out states will be rendered to the R.S.M. who will render complete state to the Adjutant on parade

8 TRANSPORT
Transport will march in rear of the Battalion.

C.S. Wilkins

Lieut. & A/ Adjutant.
1st. Battalion The Bedfordshire Regiment.

15 INFANTRY BRIGADE.

1 BATTALION BEDFORDSHIRE
REGIMENT.

1914 AUG TO 1919 APR.

1570

15 INFANTRY BRIGADE.

1 BATTALION BEDFORDSHIRE REGIMENT.

1914 AUG TO 1919 APR.

1570

www.ingramcontent.com/pod-product-compliance
Lightning Source LLC
Chambersburg PA
CBHW081530160426
43191CB00011B/1730